The Rebooting of a Teacher's Mind

Brenda A. Dyck

NMSA

National Middle School Association
Westerville, Ohio

National Middle School Association
4151 Executive Parkway, Suite 300
Westerville, Ohio 43081
Telephone (800) 528-NMSA
web: www.nmsa.org

The author and publisher wish to thank Gary Hopkins, editor in chief, for generously granting permision to reprint these articles that originally appeared in *Education World* (http://www.education-world.com).

Printed in the United States of America.

Sue Swaim, Executive Director
Jeff Ward, Deputy Executive Director
April Tibbles, Director of Publications
Edward Brazee, Editor, Professional Publications
John Lounsbury, Consulting Editor, Professional Publications
Mary Mitchell, Designer and Editorial Assistant
Mark Shumaker, Cover Design
Dawn Williams, Production Specialist
Marcia Meade-Hurst, Senior Publications Representative

Library of Congress Cataloging-in-Publication Data
　　　Dyck, Brenda A., date
　　　　　The rebooting of a teacher's mind/Brenda A. Dyck.
　　　　　　p. cm.
　　　　　Includes bibliographical references.
　　　　　ISBN 1-56090-175-6 (pbk.)
　　　　　　1. Educational technology. 2. Effective teaching. 3. Educational
　　　　　change. 4. Middle school education. I. Title
　　　　　LB1028.3.D93 2004
　　　　　373.1102--dc22　　　　　　　　　　　　　　　　　2004058753

Table of Contents

Foreword
by Rick Wormeli

I'm sitting here at my computer downloading the latest postings to a popular middle level listserv, and it happens—Brenda Dyck's name pops up on the list. She's sent three messages. At that moment, I join the other 600 people online knowing that we're going to learn something new, for Brenda Dyck has posted!

My e-mail software program allows me to sort messages by author. Putting together all my "Brenda Dyck" messages creates a professional development experience that rivals any other. In her postings, no word is wasted, and every line advances the reader-educator with insight and practicality. Day after day, locally, and literally on the other side of the planet, Brenda opens doors and makes dreams come true. Yes, she's wise and quick with solutions to problems, but even better, she provides the tools for us to grow on our own—the consummate teacher. We're fortunate enough to be in the education profession during her time of contributions online.

Brenda is a rising voice of reason in North America and abroad. Her professionalism, creativity, and teaching savvy are shaping teachers and education—and will for decades to come. She has made connections between impoverished schools and wealthier ones, each in different cultures, bringing us closer to the kind of world in which we want to live. She's walked computer-phobic teachers through the seemingly overwhelming morass of technology integration, turning those teachers' classrooms into the living promise of what modern teaching can be, given the right tools and training. She's also opened her heart and practice to the close scrutiny of her colleagues. We've seen the practical teaching dilemmas from her practice followed by the frontline, real-time inspiration found in her solutions. There are only a handful of people who have this wide-ranging, positive impact on teachers and students, and Brenda's one of them.

The Rebooting of a Teacher's Mind is the book we've been waiting for Brenda to write. In this compilation, containing many articles written previously, Brenda reflects current best practices in education. The best part of the book is her humanity. She shows us her struggles and triumphs on a variety of fronts, allowing us to see her development as a reflective practitioner—one of the trademarks of a highly accomplished teacher, according to the National Board for Professional Teaching Standards. She's not afraid to share lessons that bombed, or to celebrate when something goes well. Vicariously, we learn and grow with her.

As her introduction shows, Brenda is a risk taker. In this day of public accounting for high quality teaching, taking risks in the classroom is not for the faint of heart. She shows us how to push the envelope with courage born of sound pedagogy and deep conviction, while protecting the goals of the school in which she serves. She makes a spirited case for reforming our thinking about teaching and learning, one teacher at a time, or many at a time. The idea is to keep asking, "Why do we do things this way?" or "What would happen if we tried it this other way?" She's aware of how many of us may be pushed beyond our comfort zones with such explorations, but that is her point—to shed complacency and reveal the possible.

In the section on teachers, Brenda jump-starts our enthusiasm for sharing our world with students. She explores how to put fun into learning, including how to keep students and ourselves interested in those last waning weeks of the school year. There are more reflective topics here, too, as she explores the roles of teachers during difficult times, beating the mid-winter slump we all experience, and how to care for our physical and emotional selves. Insights about relating to students is a theme, as is the importance of taking charge of our own professional development and remaining open to transformative experiences.

In another section, Brenda gives us the tools to understand and embrace the differences among our students. She helps us see the positive in curious minds, provoking her students to look beyond the basic facts, as well as how to listen for greatness. She describes students not just as beneficiaries, but as nurturers for each other and for us, too. She also offers wisdom on dealing with students' disinterest, service projects, and how parenthood can help a person become a better teacher. Brenda's section on teachers reading aloud in non-language arts classes will be a great affirmation for many readers that this is time well spent in all subject areas. She ends the section with a reminder to see our students' future selves in their current bodies—that they are capable people, worth every moment we spend teaching them.

"Learning and Change" is another insightful section. Here, Brenda takes on homework, math education, assessment, and those who would mire us in 1960s models of school reform. She offers some great innovations from her practice, including the Reading Café, student-led Back-to-School Night, and students learning how to evaluate themselves and each other. Her practical side comes through clearly in her discussions of creative and data-driven decision making, how to simplify assignments for students, and how to reduce paperwork.

Though there are great ideas in the first three sections, her strongest section is on technology. Here, she shares her discoveries about using technology to teach standards and unleash the hidden potential of her students—all while remaining practical for teachers just starting the journey. Brenda shares the connections she and her students make across the world through her telecollaborative projects, including several poignant moments that make you glad you're a teacher. Her telementoring of Gonzalo, a 16-year-old student in Argentina, gives readers the good kind of chills—our amazing future has arrived. Though Gonzalo wasn't one of her students, his sincere interest in her "Beyond Wild Justice" telecollaborative project compelled Brenda to work with him without her seeing it as a sacrifice on her part. She did it for the chance to reach a student, to grow herself, and to navigate uncharted waters. The story gives teachers hope in humanity and what lies ahead.

The technology section continues with clear evidence for the great things that can be achieved through technology integration in core subjects. Her projects for the Global Schoolhouse CyberFair are models for others, and she gives readers multiple URLs to join the excitement. She also offers ways for educators to become "wired" to the world, and she explains how to make sure technology integration in classrooms doesn't just "glitterize" lessons, but remains focused on substantive learning—a timely discussion.

If we're lucky, *The Rebooting of a Teacher's Mind* will be the first of many books to come from her hand. Socrates was right when he said that all thinking begins with wonder. Brenda is right in there with the best minds in education, making us wonder, and even better, getting us to think for having wondered. What a boost to educators everywhere!

Rick is a National Board Certified teacher, a columnist for NMSA's *Middle Ground* magazine, and author of two acclaimed books, *Meet Me in the Middle* and *Day One & Beyond*. He lives with his family in Herndon, Virginia, where he is studying for a doctorate in science and literacy from Virginia Tech University.

X ••••

Introduction

*Reboot: (v) To turn a computer off and then on again; to restart
the operating system.* —The American Heritage Dictionary

There were those who thought I was nuts. Me, a technology-challenged
44-year-old teacher who hadn't taught since the late '70s, taking on a
teaching position at a progressive, technology-focused school. What was I
thinking?

To be honest, there was a lure of adventure to this teaching assignment.
I decided to begin with hands wide open, ready to learn anything I needed
to learn from anyone who would teach me. This was the first step in
rebooting my teaching mind!

If rebooting means to turn off and start again then this is a fine
metaphor to describe the integration of a teacher of the 1970s into the 21st
century classroom. Returning to the classroom after an 18-year absence
to raise my children, I found myself in a learning environment totally
restructured by the technology revolution and an atmosphere driven by
high accountability.

Initially, the computers posed the biggest threat to me, but ironically
it was the technology itself that guided me through the steps of rebooting
my mind. Not only did it lead me to powerful professional development
resources, it connected me with "on the grow" teachers from afar who
mentored me through those first wobbly steps of becoming a 21st century
teacher. The Internet also provided me with a venue to practice my
newfound improvement strategy—reflective writing. Writing about my
classroom practices and observations helped me clarify my thinking and
work out my questions. In the beginning these thoughts were housed
in professional portfolios, but the rebooting of my mind took on new
dimensions when I joined a vigorous, reform-minded listserv called
MiddleWeb. Together listserv members examined issues I had never even
thought about, and my reflective writing moved from my professional
portfolio onto the World Wide Web and then back into my classroom
practices where I began to flesh out what I was learning. This process
translated into an interesting bounce-catch action, one originating in a
rebooted mind and taking flight in the classroom.

In the spring of 2001, Gary Hopkins, editor of *Education World* e-
zine, e-mailed me about one of my listserv postings, and we discussed the
possibility of my submitting an article on teacher burnout to *Education*

World. "Catching Up With Our Bodies: Reflections on Teacher Burnout," became the first of a stream of articles for *Education World.* Viewing myself as a reflective practitioner positioned me to take notice of ordinary occurrences that happened in the classroom and gave me a powerful tool to improve my practice as a teacher.

In *The Rebooting of a Teacher's Mind,* renewing is a recurring theme. Each article provides the reader with a vantage point from which to observe me examining age-old classroom realities such as homework, classroom management, how teachers perceive their students, student disinterest, competition among staff, and other commonly held beliefs in education. Albert Einstein observed that, "The world we have created is a product of our thinking. It cannot be changed without changing our thinking." These articles are written in a spirit of examination and seek to uncover more relevant ways of looking at common classroom practices and attitudes. The writing doesn't just focus on changing what teachers do in the classroom, it suggests that meaningful educational reform will only be found as we reconsider the "why" behind our teaching practices and whether what we do and think is congruent with the new breed of learner that comes into our classroom each day. As a conduit, I hope I voice some of the same questions my colleagues ask because I believe that it is in talking about these questions that we'll find answers or improvements to benefit the students we teach.

While these articles, which were written over three years, are reflective, they also are ultimately intended to be a practical resource for teachers. Because of this you will see a number of hyperlinks throughout the articles as well as additional resources at the end of each article. **Please note that every link may be directly accessed at National Middle School Association's Web site** *http://www.nmsa.org/services/online/rebooting.html.*

I have identified four areas that have undergone rebooting in my own practice:

1. **Learning and Change**. Rebooting can be uncomfortable as we sift out or rework practices that are irrelevant or incompatible in a 21st century classroom.

2. **Students**. Rebooting challenges us to reconsider what our students are capable of.

3. **Teachers**. Rebooting can be empowering as we rethink our purpose and learn how to build collaborative partnerships with colleagues.

4. **Technology**. Rebooting challenges us to explore how to integrate emerging technologies to improve learning.

It is said that you know you have become fluent in a new language when you begin to think and dream in that language. I must be on my way to fluency because not only am I able to use the language but I have begun to envision and create learning opportunities that capture the essence of the language. It has become more comfortable for me to integrate the old wisdom into the new learning. But the biggest indicator of assimilation has been that I have actually started to dream in this new language. These dreams actually happen while I'm awake, and they involve creating meaningful learning opportunities for students of all ability levels, using not just new language but new ways of thinking.

As I've rebooted my teaching mind, I have a newly assimilated way of seeing and thinking about learning. The thinking and seeing is far more important than just paying lip service to the language because it is in the thinking that new avenues of learning and application will result.

When I think of how technology is changing education I am reminded of President John F. Kennedy's words as he announced his country's efforts to land a man on the moon:

> *We choose to go to the moon...not because it is easy, but because it is hard....Because that challenge is one we are willing to accept, one we are unwilling to postpone, and one we intend to win.*

> —Address at Rice University, September 12, 1962

I. Learning and Change

*L*earning and change are inseparable, learning changes you ... change
requires learning; they are two aspects of the same continuum.
Learning, in turn, is achieved as we acquire new knowledge and skills.

—W. G. Allen

1.

Peer Assessment Teaches Students How to Think

I believe there's value in students' not knowing what they don't know. When they are unaware of their limitations, they are more apt to attempt the impossible—because it seems within their reach!

Recently, I watched a group of students take on the role of peer evaluators as they applied a complicated rubric to four international technology projects from the Global Schoolhouse CyberFair competition. No one told them they might be in over their heads—so they attacked this task with the finesse of seasoned teachers.

Why put them through it?

I had several objectives in mind when I volunteered my students as peer evaluators. Over the past few years, in an effort to encourage my students to take ownership of their learning, I have provided several opportunities for them to chart their progress and evaluate their learning outcomes. My first attempts were as simple as having students keep track of "on-time" performance. They charted their ability to manage daily homework and hand in assignments on time. At the same time, they tracked the issues that interfered with their meeting deadlines. At report card time, students turned their data into a colorful graph that could be used to support discussions about any possible connection between incomplete assignments and report card marks. They discovered that the data told a story; it provided us with information we might use to plan improvement strategies.

More recently, my students have kept track of a series of quizzes on fractions. I had them do this so I could see whether they had the ability to retain the slippery skills of adding and subtracting fractions and to show them how teachers use data to plan strategies for success. I purposely increased the length of time between quizzes so that we could determine whether learning lasted over an extended period of time. Realizing that, with guidance, students were quite capable of interpreting graphed outcomes turned out to be a defining moment for me. This revelation enabled me to take the next step in their learning process.

Moving from self-assessment to peer assessment

When I heard that Global Schoolhouse was interested in using peer evaluators for the CyberFair 2002 competition, I jumped at the opportunity. I decided this would be a great place for my grade seven students to familiarize themselves with the criteria on which quality online projects were judged and to hone their developing evaluation skills.

After registering my class as peer evaluators, we received a list of four projects. Two of the projects came from Canada, one came from the Philippines, and one was from students in Singapore. We spent several periods acquainting ourselves with the 11-page rubric; we discussed the evaluation categories and did a practice run on an unrelated online project. On evaluation day, I assigned a category to students and sent them off to begin their work.

Can they do it?

There was an air of seriousness as students applied the rubric criteria to each of the four projects. I could almost hear brain gears grinding as they tried to decide whether a 3 or a 4 should be assigned to a descriptor on the rubric. This dilemma opened up the opportunity to talk about what might constitute a 3 or a 4. On several occasions, I had to remind myself that I was having a discussion about assessment—using the language of assessment—with a group of 13-year-olds.

It was interesting to watch a group of *experts* emerge from this motley crew of evaluators. It was easy to identify the writing wizards by their natural affinity for editing the content for grammar, spelling, and sentence structure. Artistic students naturally pointed out such visual weaknesses as color choice or lack of balance. Technology experts addressed overuse of Flash, slow-loading pages, and the html problems that only they understood.

My newfound respect for my students' abilities to assess was not, however, shared by the students themselves. During our debriefing activity, several expressed discomfort with the perceived "power" they felt when marking a project into which someone had obviously put so much effort. I guess it's not easy to make the transition from student to evaluator in the space of one day!

Additional Resources

What Happened Between Assessments? *
http://www.masters.ab.ca/bdyck/Assessment/index.htm

Take a look at how a group of grade six students were challenged to think as evaluators as they worked on a fractions unit.

The Global Schoolhouse
http://www.gsh.org/

This Web site provides online opportunities for teachers to collaborate, communicate, and celebrate shared learning experiences.

International Schools CyberFair
http://www.gsh.org/cf/index.html

Read about the largest educational event of its kind ever held on the Internet. The program has brought together more than 500,000 students from more than 75 countries.

CyberFair's Peer Evaluation Process
http://www.gsh.org/cf/rubric/index.html

An introduction to peer review and a detailed rubric students used to evaluate projects submitted to CyberFair.

*To access the URLs in *The Rebooting of a Teacher's Mind,* go to:
http://www.nmsa.org/services/online/rebooting.html

Please note that Internet Web sites are often not permanent. Some of the sites in this book may expire or become inactive. If you find such a site, simply go to another address or enter your keyword into a search engine such as Google (www.google.com) and select a new site.

2.

When Molding Minds Gets Messy

To be a teacher, we are told, is to be a *molder of minds.* I am quite comfortable with that label—as long as it revolves around safe activities, such as teaching basic information, planning innovative lessons, and keeping track of student progress. That kind of molding is concrete and can be carried out without much risk.

Being a molder of minds, however, becomes more sobering when I consider the potential I have to shape or bias the attitudes and opinions of my students. The realization that, because of my position at the front of the classroom, my daily instruction can oversimplify complex issues or sway student opinion is a daunting consideration for me.

When the molding gets messy

Influencing young minds was never such a concern as it was during the first few months of 2003 while the world held its breath to see if America would go to war with Iraq and then witnessed the first attacks. Like many other teachers, I worked out my own position on this issue, and as I weighed the pros and cons of going to war, I realized what a complicated issue this was and how ill-equipped I felt to make a judgment.

How glad I am to teach in a time that recognizes the fact that teachers don't have all the answers—that the best way we can help to illuminate the truth for our students is by presenting all sides of an issue and allowing our students to develop their own opinions!

Moving from messy to meaning

Many great tools and resources are available to help facilitate meaningful, unbiased classroom discussions that

- Engage as many students as possible
- Cultivate a climate that respects diversity and the right to voice opinions and ideas
- Ask students thought-provoking questions from alternative perspectives
- Challenge students' opinions by asking them to support their views
- Help students organize and analyze their thinking through the use of graphic organizers—such as

- —Venn diagrams
  http://www.venndiagram.com

- —interrelationship charts
  http://www.uvm.edu/~auditwww/tools/interrel.html?tp+true

- —fishbone and bone diagrams
  http://www.middleweb.com/MWLresources/dyckarticle1.html

- —process charts
  http://www.masters.ab.ca/bdyck/Rights/rrprocess.pdf

- Utilize debate to disclose both sides of an issue
  http://www.educationworld.com/a lesson/lesson304.shtml

- Make use of simulations that transport students into the situations or issues being studied
  http://www.education-world.com/a_curr/curr391.shtml

Rarely do we have such a unique opportunity to apply critical thinking skills within an authentic task as we do in discussing the war in Iraq. While it may be tempting to use the classroom to vent a given point of view, how wise it is for us to remember the sacred trust we hold as teachers. Events such as these offer a perfect opportunity to use our position to equip students with thinking skills that will support them for the rest of their lives. In doing that, we provide the ultimate learning experience. We help students make personal meaning out of chaos—meaning that will translate into ownership and, we hope, into future action by our students.

Who knows? Maybe one of us will mold the mind that holds the answer to world peace.

Additional Resources

The Decision To Go To War: Critical Analysis and Role Play

http://www.pbs.org/newshour/extra/teachers/lessonplans/iraq/war.html

High school teacher Laura Maupin offers this powerful role-play activity.

Teaching Is for Thinking

http://www.ncrel.org/he/tot/think.htm

Among the resources you will find here are scripts that will help you see how a teacher learned to step back and let the thinking begin *http://www.ncrel.org/he/tot/think/script33.htm* and how a teacher improved classroom discussions.

http://www.ncrel.org/he/tot/think/script46.htm
http://www.ncrel.org/he/tot/think/script23.htm

Liberating Minds

http://www.ascd.org/readingroom/edupdate/1998/1aug.html

Help your students take charge of their thinking.

3.

Learning Made Simple

Did you hear about the old woman who spent a week in a shopping mall because she couldn't find her way out? She bought food during the day and slept on a bench at night. Being a spatially challenged person, I find this scenario quite plausible. I have felt disoriented in facilities that apparently made sense to those who planned their layouts. When you don't know where you are, you might feel panicky, frustrated, or embarrassed.

As an educator, I make a living helping students maneuver through the "malls" of learning. Some students breeze along with a seemingly natural sense of direction. They need little assistance in sorting through the learning expectations given to them daily. However, I also see students who struggle with how to reach their learning goals or students who are downright confused by what teachers ask of them. Teachers, myself included, often mistakenly assume students "just know" what we want them to do. We create procedures or goals that have little meaning to students. Like those shopping mall planners, we create them without thinking through all the problems our students might face in understanding them.

I recall a number of the assignments my children have brought home over the years. Not only were the instructions vague but they were often asked to carry out tasks that required skills that had not yet been taught. Working with them at home proved to be a case of "the blind leading the blind" as I tried to direct them toward successful completion of each assignment. I found myself teaching skills such as the business letter format, how to summarize research, and how to prepare for an upcoming test. I often wondered why I, as a parent, was teaching those skills and if anyone had given any thought to the directions provided for students.

In a moment of honest reflection, I considered the possibility that my students and parents might feel the same way about my assignments. My reflection prompted me to experiment with ways to better explain skills and procedures that had proved too complex for my students to grasp. I forced myself to dissect the directions and assignments I had given and to exclude from them anything that was nonessential to core learning.

Following are brief descriptions of some of the tools I implemented as a result of my reflection on the student assignments I gave:

Assignment Sheets. I had always been frustrated by the discrepancy between my assignment expectations and the resulting student work. Cognizant of the fact that many of my students were missing important parts of my verbal directions, I prepared detailed assignment sheets that stated—in checklist format—each of my assignment benchmarks. (Find a link to a sample assignment sheet at the end of this article.) I encouraged learners to check the box next to each benchmark as they included it in their work. Students found it useful to see how I intended to mark the assignment. Providing students with the assignment and assessment sheets up front informed students about what I expected and how I planned to mark it. That eliminated the guesswork for my students; it also helped students produce work that was closer to the assignment standard.

Working Papers. The "working paper," another support tool I developed, walked my students through the steps of their writing assignments. The tool reminded them of specific elements to include. (See links to sample working papers on page 15.) Working papers provided a model for disorganized writers; they broke down tasks into manageable steps for students who were immobilized by the immensity of an assignment. Working papers doubled as evidence of the students' writing process.

Graphic Organizers. These powerful thinking tools enabled my students to see where they were and where they were going. I created graphic organizers, which I called "process charts," to clearly demonstrate for students

- The steps in performing long division
- How to successfully complete a science fair project
- The steps needed to achieve a career goal
- A way to follow the plot of a story
- What needs to be done to ready the classroom for end-of-day dismissal.

Flashcards. Placing the main bytes of information from a unit of study on flashcards provided students with a practical review tool that helped keep the important facts fresh in their memories. This ongoing tool was especially useful for getting a handle on the extensive vocabulary that is part of science, social studies, and language curricula.

Additional Resources

Assignment Sheet
http://www.occdsb.on.ca/~proj1615/leaders/custom2.html

This is a sample "assignment sheet" from one of my online projects.

The following links will take you to pages that offer sample "working papers" that I have used in the classroom and a sample assessment sheet. You will need *Adobe Acrobat* to read the files.

Working Paper 1
http://www.occdsb.on.ca/~proj1615/leaders/workingpaper.pdf

Working Paper 2
http://www.occdsb.on.ca/~proj1615/leaders/workingpaper.pdf

Working Paper 3
http://www.occdsb.on.ca/~proj1615/paper.pdf

Assessment Sheet
http://www.occdsb.on.ca/~proj1615/leaders/assesssheet.pdf

Edward de Bono Personal Site
http://www.edwarddebono.com/

This Web site offers information about the work of Edward de Bono, a leading authority in the field of human thinking.

Graphic Organizers
http://www.ncrel.org/sdrs/areas/issues/students/learning/lr1grorg.htm

Browse through a number of graphic tools designed to support student learning.

4.

Homework: A Place for Rousing Reform

It was exactly a year ago when my vice-principal came to our team and announced that we would re-evaluate our homework policy. With plenty of negative feedback regarding homework, we were asked to consider

- What constituted appropriate homework
- The amount of time students spent on homework
- A communication system that would track how much homework each teacher assigned
- The value, relevance, process, and clarity of homework assignments and project work.

I clearly remember the negative body language exhibited by the teachers upon receiving that message. (I'm sure my body language was no different!) I recall the begrudging attitude we brought to the assignment. We didn't believe our homework expectations were out of line. We *liked* the wonderful projects we were assigning. And we couldn't imagine getting through the curriculum without the assistance of homework.

The process of shapeshifting

During the next two months we discovered a truth about education reform:

The better the idea, the more resistance it will stir up.

As much as we resisted changing our homework approaches, as we discussed the purpose of homework we discovered a number of outdated mental models existed among us. With hesitation, we began to question our homework practices—and even our favorite assignments. We were *shapeshifting.*

Our shapeshifting adventure led us to consider the changes that had occurred in families in recent years. We thought about all the single-parent families, the working moms, and the students who were deeply involved in ballet or hockey or other activities. We realized that many students did homework in a very unsupportive environment or in the car on the way to piano lessons.

Reflecting on the homework we were assigning helped us see that our assignments were sometimes unclear or complicated; students had difficulty making sense of assignment expectations when working on them at home, and the assignments were often confusing for parents as well. Equipped with this new understanding, we began to restructure our assignment expectations. That resulted in improved assignment sheets with clearer benchmarks and rubrics.

We also discussed whether students were doing the homework assignments alone or with parents' help. Did we really *know* that the work we were marking was an accurate reflection of our students' knowledge and ability? As a result of *that* question, we decided to start having larger parts of written assignments done in class so teachers could observe the thinking and writing process in action.

Finally, we discussed whether lengthy projects—some of which took several weeks to complete—merited the time and effort involved. We evaluated what learning actually took place and whether the same learning could occur with less time-intensive assignments. The result was that many of us gave up favorite assignments. No one mandated it, but honest evaluation forced us to admit that some of our assignments amounted to a lot of fluff.

Shapeshifting can be messy

As shapeshifters, we debated—and sometimes even argued. No practices were sacred. It became common for us to challenge each other's thinking. We were on a search for relevant truth, and changes in homework policy resulted. For the rest of the year, homework tension among teachers, students, and parents was not an issue.

What my colleagues and I learned along the way didn't have as much to do with homework as it did with discovering how to implement meaningful change by reshaping the learning environment. This *shapeshifting*, we discovered, could be a messy and exciting process—but well worth the effort!

Additional Resources

Homework Takes a Hit
http://www.educationworld.com/a_issues/issues134.shtml

Education World takes a thorough look at the homework issue.

Put an End to Homework Horror!
http://www.education-world.com/a_curr/curr306.shtml

Education World interviews author Nancy Paulu who examines ways to make homework more productive.

End Homework Now
http://www.ascd.org/readingroom/edlead/0104/kralovec.html

The authors of *The End of Homework: How Homework Disrupts Families, Overburdens Children, and Limits Learning* discuss the end of homework and other education reforms.

The Homework Burden
http://www.pbs.org/newshour/bb/education/july-dec00/homework.htm

This insightful article by Betty Ann Browser focuses on the homework debate.

Author Argues Amount of Homework Adds Pressure on Kids
http://detnews.com/2000/schools/0010/13/e06e-133319.htm

This article from the *Detroit News* suggests that homework can put pressure on students.

5.

Fighting the 1960s Mental Models
of the Perfect Classroom

That old familiar feeling surfaces each time I tackle an activity-based project with my students. Although I am committed to implementing hands-on learning, I have a secret fear that a visitor will wander in during a moment of constructive chaos. My apprehension seems connected to a nagging feeling that a quiet, orderly classroom is the trademark of a good teacher. That feeling is probably related to my own learning memories of students working at desks in orderly rows, peace and quiet, and a teacher, of course, in complete control—seeing everything, knowing everything. That image, circa 1965, is deeply ingrained as my idea of a perfect on-track classroom.

I struggle with some of those same feelings when I picture myself as a mom. In my mind's eye I envision having warm cookies for my children after school, laundry that is under control, a clean and orderly house, and time to knit or sew for my family. I imagine being relaxed enough to listen to my children's stories.

Yesterday once more?

Those mental models of teaching and motherhood plague me; they describe the mom I grew up with and the home I grew up in. Having one foot in each generation is a slippery place to be! I've often wondered if it is possible to reconcile our past mental models with the current reality of our profession and our private roles as women. Whenever my thoughts take that path, I try to get back on track.

First of all, I must remember that recreating the classroom of the 1960s will not prepare my students for the world I will launch them into. Even if I would feel more comfortable there, I remind myself that I am developing a learning culture that promotes questioning, exploration, and collaboration. Why? Because my students will not just need to "know," they will need to be able to apply what they know. They will not just need to read about solutions, they will need to come up with solutions. And they will need to be equipped with the ability to work with others as they do these things.

Teaching students how to function in a collaborative environment won't happen in rows of desks in a silent, non-interactive classroom.

Questioning and problem solving won't happen without dialogue, and dialogue doesn't happen in a silent, teacher-controlled classroom. In today's classrooms, teachers are not only knowledge imparters; they are co-learners with their students.

The classroom experiences my students need don't happen in isolation. They happen in a vibrant, moving, dynamic environment—an environment that is sometimes noisy, messy, and slightly chaotic. At times, I even feel a little unsure of what might happen next. In spite of its dynamic nature, however, that environment is not disorganized, out of control, or void of respect.

I need to remember the same things when I consider my parenting benchmarks. No, there may not always be cookies fresh out of the oven or clean socks in the drawer. My children, however, have become co-participants in the home, just as my students have in the classroom. I'm not the only one who can clean a toilet or put dinner on the table. Out of this arrangement will come kids with skill sets for life—unlike me, who didn't know how to clean a bathroom when I got married.

Emphasis on communication and relationships will sometimes pre-empt knitting and sewing at home and perfect 1960s orderliness in the classroom, but I know it is "talk-time" that will shape our children into who they need to become.

Additional Resource

A Summary of New Learning Paradigms
http://www.utexas.edu/courses/svinicki/382L/summary.html

An education class from the University of Texas looks at shifts in teaching and learning.

6.

Digging Beneath the Surface of Assessment

Updating my education paradigm has kept me hopping! Just when I am confident that I am certain about what I know, someone challenges my thinking. This time it happened in math class.

One thing I've always liked about teaching math is the concrete nature of the subject. There are definite skills to teach, tests to give, and quantitative test results to record. Equipped with this cognitive data, I am usually confident that I have an accurate handle on the learning profile of each of my students. This overconfidence lasted until I read the investigative article "What Can Student Drawings Tell Us About High-Stakes Testing in Massachusetts?" by Anne Wheelock, Damian Bebell, and Walt Haney.

Using art to assess math

The premise of Wheelock's study is that anxiety can interfere with student learning. The study used a drawing activity as the jumping-off point to assess students' affective learning—their feelings, emotions, and perceptions related to high-stakes testing. Students in grades 4, 8, and 10 were asked to draw themselves in a test-taking situation. Teachers then applied a coding scheme and analyzed the content of the drawings. They were looking for reactions to test content, format, length, and difficulty. Indicators of feelings, emotions, or hints to how students viewed themselves as mathematical learners were observed as well.

Most educators are aware that math anxiety is alive and well in many classrooms. My own mathematical learning was full of stress and embarrassment. As a math teacher, I am very cognizant that many students enter my class each year dragging a great deal of math baggage. Aware that fear and anxiety can short-circuit learning, I decided to replicate the drawing activity documented in Wheelock's study. My objective was to observe the affective side of learning so I could add an enhanced dimension of accuracy and depth to my math students' learning profiles.

My students' artwork provided a diverse view of their experiences in math testing settings. Every picture told a story. Some interesting elements jumped out of their test-taking art.

- I saw a wide variety of body postures—some students sat up straight and confident, some sprawled desperately across the top of the desk in a face-plant position, some jumped for joy, some sat with sagging shoulders, and some sat passively with hands folded.

- I observed an assortment of facial expressions—I saw a look of glee, a furrowed brow, a smug look, rolling eyes, and perplexed, pained, or spacey expressions.
- Many students included thought bubbles in the drawings. The test-taking thoughts included "That was easy!" "What is 39 X 24?! Oh wait...it is 930...no...it is 936!" "Think, think, think! How much time do I have left??" "I hope I do good!" and "Help!"
- I spotted an abundance of question marks on student artwork. One girl completely covered the background of her page with question marks.
- A number of students placed a clock in a prominent place in their pictures.

So now what?

The first step in any assessment process is gathering cognitive data—but the art activity was *only* the first step toward building student learning profiles. The next, equally important step is to take the time to explore the significance of emotions and feelings that students bring to their learning. Where should I go from here? That is the question that should be asked at the end of any assessment process. What changes could be made in my classroom climate that will take into consideration the stresses expressed in my students' pictures? Dealing with those questions may be just as important as how I teach the curriculum skills.

Additional Resources

Using Art To Assess Math

http://mathart.freeservers.com/

"Draw yourself in a test-taking situation" was my instruction to my students. This Web page displays two pages of my students' artwork.

What Can Student Drawings Tell Us About High-Stakes Testing in Massachusetts?

http://www.aasa.org/publications/ln/00-12/00-12-01draw.htm

Read Anne Wheelock's thought-provoking study. Included are a series of prompts that might be used to help students reflect on their thinking and learning.

Coding Matrix

http://www.tcrecord.org/RestrictedAccess.asp?/Content.asp?ContentID-10634

Access the coding matrix that can be used to interpret student work. You will need to register in order to access the document, but it is free.

7.

Driven By Data: What It's Like to Teach in the Age of Accountability

Fighting data asphyxiation is difficult but possible. —William Van Winkle

This week I'm neck deep in data analysis, sorting through the results from a beginning-of-the-year math assessment. For me, this isn't a comfortable place to be because I am not a statistician. I even wonder if I will know what to do with the information once I get it!

Since I am an educator in the Age of Accountability, I resign myself to gathering and analyzing everything from classroom behavior to achievement test results and homework completion. But as I wade through the rows and rows of numbers in front of me, I speculate whether the time I'm spending will justify the time I'm *not* spending creating new and engaging curriculum, developing meaningful relationships with my students, providing feedback on assignments, or even applying new learning applications.

Once I finish the lengthy process of gathering, plotting, and looking for meaning in the data, a question lingers: *How will I convert this information into an improvement plan for students?*

Simplifying the process

I realize how easy it is to drown in an excess of information and analysis, so I've sought out a number of online tools that have empowered me to investigate and evaluate student learning and classroom issues in a quick, uncomplicated manner:

- Test-creation Web sites such as Quia *http://www.quia.com/* and online survey sites like Zoomerang *http://www.zoomerang.com* help me streamline the data collection process. Those tools help me analyze the results and turn them into easy-to-read graphs.

- The free graphing tool *http://nces.ed.gov/nceskids/graphing/* on the National Center for Education Statistics' Web page for kids *http://nces.ed.gov/nceskids/graphing/*. That tool provides easy-to-use templates for communicating information visually.

- Graphic organizers *http://www.writedesignonline.com/organizers/* to help me identify key issues, set targets, and create a plan for implementing the results of the data.

When is enough enough?

> *In the information age, there can be too much exposure and too much information and too much sort of quasi-information. ...There's a danger that too much stuff cramming in on people's minds is just as bad for them as too little in terms of the ability to understand, to comprehend.*
> — Bill Clinton

When it comes to data analysis, I have to resist buying into the old adage that "more is better." Before I yield to yet another data collection activity, my experience this fall collecting data related to the start-of-the-year math assessment reminds me that I need to employ a number of screening questions to determine if the effort will be worth it:

- What is the purpose of collecting these data? What question am I seeking to answer?
- How will these data help me improve instruction?
- What information will help me answer these questions?
- What is the most time-efficient way of collecting and analyzing this information?
- Who needs to participate?
- What is a reasonable amount of time to devote to gathering and analyzing?
- What teaching, personal activities, and responsibilities will I have to put on hold in order to explore this question?
- Do I have the time and resources available to me to apply the outcomes of this study?

I have to remember that it's always more enjoyable to start another study than to use the data I already have, and those questions will help me determine whether new data are really needed. Those questions will help me create some parameters so my priorities stay in balance—so data collection and analysis don't happen at the expense of essential one-on-one time with my students.

Additional Resources

Deep Thinking and Deep Reading in an Age of Info-Glut, Info-Garbage, Info-Glitz, and Info-Glimmer

http://www.fno.org/mar97/deep.html

A thought-provoking article from Jamie McKenzie.

Informing Ourselves to Death

http://world.std.com/~jimf/informing.html

Leave it to education thinking guru Neil Postman to put information technology in its place!

8.
A New Spin On Back-to-School Night

I have vivid memories of Back-to-School Night 1961. My classmates and I had spent that afternoon constructing life-size replicas of ourselves from large brown grocery bags. All of us giggled at the thought of our parents walking into a classroom filled with paper-bag children sitting at their desks. We had coyly told our parents at dinner that we too would be attending Back-to-School Night.

Unfortunately, those paper-bag replicas would be the closest any of us would ever come to actually attending Back-to-School Night because, in those days, those special evenings took place in the adult world—a place where children were not invited.

Like many other sacred cows of the teaching profession, Back-to-School Nights are undergoing a facelift. Educators are re-examining their purpose and relevance and wondering how to entice parents to attend. Those were among the considerations that led my school to rethink Back-to-School Night. We ended up enlisting the help of those who have plenty of relevant things to say about what goes on in our classrooms—our students.

Student-led back-to-school nights

In this new paradigm, students have become the key players in the events of Back-to-School Night. This special evening has shifted from an event that students only heard about secondhand to a special opportunity for them to take the lead. Back-to-School Night now offers teachers a unique opportunity to teach communication, organization, and leadership skills that will serve students throughout their lives. This start-of-the-year event also offers students an early opportunity to develop and demonstrate their growing self-confidence.

In this new vision of Back-to-School Night, students play a major role in planning and carrying out the night's events. They begin by working with their teachers to identify the key learning components of their classrooms. Each component is assigned a number and listed in a "classroom tour brochure" that students prepare. That brochure is a collaborative effort; students create artwork, write descriptions, type text into the computer, and help fold the completed brochures.

The brochure my students created included descriptions of classroom areas such as

- The overhead that projects a "Do Now" activity on the wall
- A bulletin board display of our class motto
- Our portfolio and reading corner
- A display of the texts and novel studies that will be covered during the year
- A display of student writing
- A computer screen opened to our Schoolnotes.com *http:// www.schoolnotes.com* Web site
- A computer screen displaying a Zoomerang *http:// www.zoomerang.com* survey that polls parents on their Grade Six Knowledge Quotient.

In preparation for the parent tour, we discussed the purpose or use of each area or activity described in the brochure; we shared presentation suggestions; and we anticipated questions parents might have or snags we might encounter. Students practiced with their peers, and everyone worked together to ready the room for the evening. By the time we were finished with our preparations, the whole process was running like a well-oiled machine.

A "living" back-to-school night

That night, as students entered the classroom with their parents, they morphed into tour guides. I was the proverbial fly on the wall. I stood back and watched students take the driver's seat. I listened as they described their learning environment to their parents. They performed their newly discovered leadership roles with confidence and enthusiasm as parents followed along behind. I could tell from the expressions on parents' faces that they were clearly impressed with their children's abilities to lead; most had never seen their children take on that role before.

This year, "meeting the teacher" took a back seat on Back-to-School Night. In place of that old standby, the students took on responsibility for describing their firsthand knowledge of their school day and learning.

Those paper-bag students of my school days have been retired for good, but they came to life on Back-to-School Night 2004.

9.
The Little Reading Café

E ach Thursday afternoon, my grade six classroom undergoes a face-lift. We turn the lights down low and light candles. Comfortable pillows appear on the floor, strains of jazz or baroque music float through the air, and students snuggle up with their books. Quietly, someone passes around cookies, doughnuts, or brownies. Readers nod their thanks and return to their books. Some students sip on mugs of tea or hot chocolate. All of us experience 45 minutes of bliss in the middle of an active school day!

It wasn't always that way. Four years ago, I knew I had to look for different ways to get my students engaged in reading. It troubled me that the majority of students I inherited each year viewed recreational reading with intense dislike. Silent reading times were anything but enjoyable as I walked around the room, making sure everyone had a book on the go. I wondered why young people who had loved to read in the earlier grades were now turning up their noses at reading.

Before I could reinvent the independent reading part of my program, I needed to identify the core purpose of this infamous institution. After much reflection, I rationalized that independent reading time was about developing a love for reading in my students—nothing more, nothing less. From there, the rest was easy. I used as my model the well-known bookstore chains such as Barnes & Noble. Those bookstores have made an art of creating an ambience that beckons people to read. The enticements of cozy chairs, interesting music, and food have helped reading become trendy once again!

Equipped with my core purpose, I moved an old couch and a chair into my classroom. I hung a few artsy posters on the walls, threw some comfy cushions on the floor, and provided music and a few candles. To that, we added food and drink; after all, the aroma of coffee is one of the most enticing things about bookstore cafes. Students take turns bringing cookies, brownies, chips, or oranges.

I knew it was important to keep our "reading café" fresh and vibrant, so I scheduled a number of special events.

- People who visit share their own love of reading. The principal, the custodian, and parents have come, books in hand, to share a favorite story.
- A local author came to explain how he published his own book.

- One of our parents read Scottish literature to the students—complete with a Scottish accent.

- On Valentine's Day, we held a "Death By Chocolate" event. All snacks were chocolate, and the students listened to an authentic, old-fashioned mystery radio drama.

- I announced special events on a poster displayed outside my classroom so it really felt like a special event was taking place!

My students and I love our "reading café" period. For me, it has been a time when I can communicate to my students my own love of reading and put feet to Galileo's words, *You cannot teach a man anything, you can only help him discover it within himself.*

Additional Resources

Lessons from Oprah, Harry Potter, and the Internet
http://www.trelease-on-reading.com/rah_chpt7_p2.html

Writer Jim Trelease explores what Oprah Winfrey and Harry Potter can teach us about reluctant readers.

The Joy of Reading: Superman and Me
http://www.fallsapart.com/superman.html

This excerpt comes from the book *The Most Wonderful Books: Writers on Discovering the Pleasures of Reading.*

Joy of Reading
http://www.fno.org/reading/read.html

Jamie MacKenzie photographs young people immersed in reading.

10.
Make Time to Teach:
Ten Tools for Reducing Paperwork

They say a teacher will never forget his or her first class. That must be true, because 30 years later, I can still picture those students' faces. I can still recite many of their names and recall many moments of learning we shared.

It is also amazing to me that, after all these years, the call in my heart to teach is as fresh as it was when I met that first class in 1974. I am as excited now as I was then when my instruction and my students' understanding collide!

An intruder in the classroom

Sadly, however, I get a sense that now an intruder threatens to sap my passion. I worry that the intruder might prevent me from putting as much energy as I can into creating lessons that energize me and engage my students. That intruder is...*paperwork.*

It seems to me that paperwork has slowly crept into my daily life at school—and now threatens to overwhelm it. With its roots firmly planted in the soil of accountability, I find I am spending more time than ever filling out forms in order to fulfill expectations from all levels of administration. Sometimes the weight of that paperwork is unbearable.

Recently, I took part in a MiddleWeb listserv *http://www.middleweb.com/* discussion, in which we talked about the mind-boggling mountain of paperwork that comes our way. The MiddleWeb teachers came up with more than 75 ways that paperwork intrudes on their lives. With all that paperwork, I wonder how teachers find the time to teach!

Even the list's chaotic background music—*The Simpson's* theme—seems to mirror the hectic pace of school, doesn't it? *http://www.masters.ab.ca/ bdyck/Professional/Paper/html*

Digging out from under

Thankfully, a handful of free online tools have come to my rescue, helping to streamline some of the most tedious paperwork tasks that get in the way of one-on-one time with my students. They have helped me bury some of the paperwork and focus on my "soul mission"—connecting with my students. Best of all, those tools enhance my instruction time by helping students reflect, organize, and think in new ways.

Learning Checklists
http://4teachers.org/projectbased/checklist.shtml

This practical learning tool scaffolds students as they learn to take responsibility for their learning. It enables me to create customized checklists that I can print for student use.

Blogs
http://www.blogger.com/

Just when you think you've seen everything, the Web comes up with another powerful learning tool! Blogs provide a place for students and teachers to "think" online—separately or together. The Blogger Web site provides space for journaling, organizational thinking, locating research sources, having classroom discussions, or even publishing student work.

RubiStar
http://rubistar.4teachers.org/

Rubistar's easy-to-use template helps teachers create curriculum-specific rubrics in a minimum amount of time. The rubrics help define assignment expectations for students, and they speed up the marking process for teachers.

Zoomerrang
http://www.zoomerang.com

This online survey tool provides a way to find out what students, parents, and peers know and think. The survey results arm educators with data to adjust and improve instruction and communication.

ThinkTank
http://thinktank.4teachers.org/

This site offers a fun way for students to create research organizers for reports and projects. It is a great tool for guiding student thinking.

Puzzlemaker
http://puzzlemaker.school.discovery.com/

This practical Web site turns word lists into customized word search, crossword, and math puzzles. Puzzles can be saved in a "custom account" to be retrieved later.

IKeepBookmarks

http://ikeepbookmarks.com/

This site not only organizes favorite Web page bookmarks, but it creates special topical folders for students to use as they research specific topics.

The Connection Cube

http://learnweb.harvard.edu/alps/thinking/reflect_activities.cfm#connection

Helping students make connections between what they already know and new learning is one of the most important things teachers do. This online tool helps students connect learning to new contexts.

Teacher Forms and Letters

http://www.teachertools.org/forms_dynam.asp

Downloadable templates are listed in four categories: Discipline, Academic, Communication, and Other.

Laura Chandler's File Cabinet

http://home.att.net/~teaching/filecab.htm

This site provides a variety of practical forms that can be used in any classroom.

11.
Put On Your (Six) Thinking Hats!

Think left and think right
and think low and think high.
Oh, the thinks you can think up
if only you try! —Dr Seuss

I am the product of an educational system that challenged students to "think harder," to "think again," and frequently, to "put our thinking caps on." Although most of us understood the message behind our teachers' directions, no one had a clue about how to power up our thinking.

With the advent of brain-based learning, fewer educators hand out meaningless thinking platitudes to their students. Instead, they direct students toward such powerful thinking tools as Edward de Bono's Six Thinking Hats *http://www.edwdebono.com/*. This colorful strategy exposes learners to six different styles of thinking and helps them look at a problem from six different perspectives.

The Six Thinking Hats approach can be used to address almost any problem-solving activity you might encounter in the classroom. Assigning each thinking style a color serves as a visual cue to help students recognize the thinking skill they are using. The six different hats students might wear, and the kinds of thinking they represent, are briefly described below:

- **White Hat**. Discuss the facts and other objective information about the problem.
- **Red Hat**. Share feelings and emotions about the issue.
- **Black Hat**. Present negative aspects, or worst case scenarios, regarding the situation.
- **Yellow Hat**. Consider positives, or advantages, of the situation.
- **Green Hat**. Consider creative ideas that come from looking at the problem in a new way.
- **Blue Hat**. Sum up all that is learned.

Posting a permanent Six Thinking Hats display *http://www.masters. ab.ca/bdyck/Hats/index.html* in your classroom will provide an ever-present thinking tool to use when you and your students tackle any kind of problem.

Dealing with disappointment

Recently, one of my colleagues had an opportunity to put the Six Thinking Hats thinking tool to use. In order to prepare students for an upcoming achievement test, a small group of students had to be pulled from a physical education class once a week to work on writing skills. Although this was a short-term arrangement, those students were upset—physical education was their favorite class, and they didn't want to miss it. The teacher, realizing that she needed "buy-in" from the students, decided it was time to look at the problem from different vantage points. Over the next 40 minutes, she deliberately led her students through a discussion that focused on the different perspectives represented by the Six Thinking Hats. By the end of the period, her students

- Were able to separate the facts from their feelings
- Had an opportunity to express their disappointment, frustration, and anger
- Learned how to recognize the positive things that could come from preparing for the writing exam
- Were able to brainstorm ways they could make their tutorial time an enjoyable experience
- Were able to summarize what they learned from this experience and envision ways to use that learning in the future.

Lessons for the teacher too

As a teacher who gets to tag along on my students' thinking journeys, I often discover nuggets of revelation as my students try on different thinking hats. Like a fly on the wall, I get to hear them express their innermost feelings, suggest innovative solutions, and discover profound insights. Just as the kids do, I often find myself changing my mind as they think aloud.

Edward de Bono suggests that we need to be thinking about "what can be," not just about "what is." Using the Six Thinking Hats frees students to move past obvious problems to creative solutions.

Additional Resources

Six Thinking Hats.
http://www.twbookmark.com/books/62/0316177911/chapter_excerpt9537.html
An excerpt from Edward de Bono's thought-provoking book.

Students Talking While Others Are Talking or Teaching.
http://www.middleweb.com/MWLresources/thinkinghats.html
Use the Six Thinking Hats to confront an age-old problem.

Turning a Sad Goodbye into a Problem-tunity.
http://www.middleweb.com/MWLresources/dyckarticle2.html
Another application of the Six Thinking Hats.

Six Hats Solves All Kinds of Issues

The following are some of the problems we have solved using Six Thinking Hats:

- Incomplete homework
- Summer school attendance
- Disagreements during administration and staff "think-tank" sessions

When trying to solve those problems and many others, the Six Thinking Hats approach has helped set the stage for a variety of viewpoints to be shared and for some uncommon solutions to be considered.

12.
Downshifting: Teaching (for Understanding) in a Lower Gear

L ike many of my colleagues, I've become proficient at "speed teaching." Speed teaching refers to our abilities to find the most time-efficient way to deliver learning to students. It is the only way to cover an ever-growing curriculum.

The passing scores in my student grade book attest to the fact that the system is working; the majority of my students are mastering the concepts and skills that their high-stakes tests will test. Or are they? The fact that I often hear my students' next year teachers complain that those who demonstrated mastery for me are woefully lacking in recall makes me wonder. Am I teaching for short-term memory or long-haul retention?

"Slow teaching"

Maurice Holt's recent *Phi Delta Kappan* article "It's Time to Start the Slow School Movement" *http://www.pdkintl.org/kappan/k0212hol.htm* reminded me of my own learning experiences during an era when it seemed teaching was more about savoring learning than just getting through it.

That article brought back memories of Mrs. Miller, my second grade teacher, who was a master at slow teaching. She was in no hurry to finish our unit on Zaire. Not only did we cover all the factual information about Zaire, we made our learning visible by creating a lifelike tabletop jungle that—to this day—I can remember constructing and watering. We watered it because we spread a thick layer of dirt across the surface of our jungle floor and excitedly buried bean seeds in the dirt and waited for them to germinate. That was in addition to building villages of stilted tribal houses set alongside the Congo River that meandered its way through the jungle! In no time, bean plants that looked strangely like jungle foliage began to poke their way through the dirt. The taller they got, the more they looked like the lofty broadleaved evergreens found in the jungles of Africa.

It's strange how memories of that tabletop jungle and what we learned that year came back to me in high school when I read Joseph Conrad's *The Heart of Darkness*. Reading Conrad's powerful description of an African jungle was like revisiting a place I had already been:

Going up that river was like traveling back to the earliest beginning of the world, where vegetation rioted on the earth and the big trees were king. An empty stream, a great silence, an impenetrable forest, the air was warm, thick, sluggish. We penetrated deeper and deeper into the heart of darkness. (Conrad, 1899)

Moving from covering to uncovering

The realization that many of my most profound learning experiences took place in slow-teaching environments has led me to try to replicate that style of instruction in my own classroom. Using multilayered topics such as children's rights, leadership, restorative justice, and homelessness as jumping off points, my students have participated in simulations, collaborated with students in other countries, and participated in debates about complex issues.

Using numerous Web resources available to me, I have had the opportunity to learn from many experts in the field of project-based learning. The George Lucas Educational Foundation Web site *http://www.glef.org/php/keyword.php?id=037* for example, provides many excellent resources that have helped me gear down my program so that students have the opportunity to develop their critical thinking skills and recapture the excitement of learning. The site's video gallery *http://www.glef.org/php/intgallery.php?id=037* has been especially helpful to me; it is a powerful archive of interviews with project-based learning experts such as Howard Gardner, Mihaly Csikszentmihalyi, and Seymour Papert.

With slow teaching my modus operandi, I realize my speed-teaching skills have not gone to waste. They still enable me to cover baseline knowledge and concepts that will ultimately free up time to lead students to become investigators, problem solvers, and innovators. Speed teaching combined with slow teaching results in establishing a learning environment where students are free to think, analyze, problem-solve, and make meaning of what they've learned.

Embracing "slow teaching" does not mean I have to settle for lower test scores; in fact, to me it's somewhat ironic that highly interactive projects and classroom practices promote academic rigor and excellence.

Additional Resources

Teaching for Understanding: Pictures of Practice
http://learnweb.harvard.edu/alps/tfu/pictures.cfm

Observe "slow teaching" in action. This Web site from ALPS (Active Learning Practice for Schools) profiles teachers who are teaching for understanding.

Teaching for Understanding: Curriculum Design Tools
http://learnweb.harvard.edu/alps/tfu/design_online.cfm

Wondering how to gear down your curriculum? Take a look at this free online tool from the Teaching for Understanding Project based at the Harvard Graduate School of Education.

Understanding Counts! Teaching for Depth in Math and Science
http://www.pz.harvard.edu/Research/MathSciMatters/BK1DPUNDRv03.pdf

How do we teach for understanding? This research paper by Tina Grotzer of the Graduate School of Education at Harvard University explores this question and how it relates to teaching math and science. (This pdf file requires Adobe Acrobat Reader.)

Horace's School: Redesigning the American High School
http://www.amazon.com/exec/obidos/tg/detail/-/0395755344/102-7208455-3816117?v=glance

A fictional portrayal of what an ideal American high school might be like, as envisioned by educator Theodore Sizer. Browse through the online excerpt.

13.
Math Class: A Time to Stand and Deliver

Math class—the very thought of it provokes fear, insecurity, even dread in a large proportion of the students who walk into our schools. Into my class they come, lugging their negative mental models about math. They act their mental models out in seemingly unrelated ways, such as appearing apathetic, acting bored, daydreaming, not doing their homework, or misbehaving.

They readily refer to themselves as kids who "just can't do math." I call them the "mathematically abused." I recognize them because I used to be one of those students myself. I spent years thinking mathematical learning was beyond my grasp. By fourth grade, I could easily identify the sound of irritation in my teacher's voice when she re-explained a concept that I continued to misunderstand. I would often say I "got it" because I knew how exasperated my math teacher would be if I didn't.

Stupid took on a very personal meaning for me in math class. I still remember the embarrassment of being asked publicly for an answer I didn't have. Even worse, I remember being asked to work out a math question on the chalkboard, knowing full well that I didn't have a clue what to do.

When I was a student, math class was something to endure. I looked forward to the day I could leave it forever!

No one is more astonished than I am that, today, I find myself *teaching* math! To my great surprise, I have discovered that I have an ability to work with students who struggle in math. I think I have that ability because I understand how stress can interfere with a student's ability to learn.

Each day, I vow that a significant amount of my teaching effort will be directed toward refurbishing my students' view of themselves as mathematical learners. Throughout the year, I employ intentional strategies directed at rebuilding my students' mathematical self-esteem. Establishing a safe environment where my students can confront their math fears and insecurities is one of my main goals.

Last spring, just before the sixth-grade achievement tests were to be administered, I decided it was time—time to share with my students the 1988 movie *Stand and Deliver*. That movie, based on a true story, is about a class of high school math students from a poor East Los Angeles area who progressed from troubled, disinterested learners into committed calculus students who sat for the AP calculus exam. Those students not only wrote the exam but in addition, all passed it!

The film moved my students immensely. It was well worth the two class periods that would have been devoted to geometric solids. In our debriefing session after the movie, we discussed various negative mental models with which my students struggled. Following are a handful of those models:

- My mom and dad weren't good at math; neither am I.
- Ability in math is related to racial or socioeconomic class.
- Once you have trouble in math, you'll always have trouble in math.
- It's the "dorky" kids who try hard at math.
- Girls will not be successful in advanced math.
- Only students who have their lives together will do well at math.
- When math gets tough, its better to just give up.
- Math is boring.
- Math teachers are boring too.

Stand and Deliver demonstrated what happens when kids don't give up. It showed what students are able to accomplish when they work hard and believe in themselves. For me, the movie spoke of the power that exists when a teacher and students truly connect; it spoke of the magical things that can happen when a teacher commits to the long haul in student learning.

Watching a movie in math class took my students by surprise since watching a movie is not really a math class thing to do. But you know what they say about unexpected learning: The unexpected is enhanced and remembered for a long time.

Additional Resources

Learning Guide for *Stand and Deliver*

http://www.teachwithmovies.org/guides/stand-and-deliver.html

A helpful guide for teachers who use the movie *Stand and Deliver* in the classroom.

Mental Models

http://www.algodonesassociates.com/planning/Mental models.pdf

This resource provides some information on the power of mental models.

Wheel of Multiple Perspectives

http://www.change-management-toolbook.com/co_06.htm

Teachers can use this tool to explore their students' mental models concerning math.

II. Students

S tudents learn what they care about... Stanford Ericksen has said, but Goethe knew something else: *In all things we learn only from those we love.* Add to that Emerson's declaration: *the secret of education lies in respecting the pupil;* and we have a formula something like this: *Students learn what they care about, from people they care about and who, they know, care about them ..."* —Barbara Harrell Carson

1.
Students Can Care and Comfort

Recently, a wave of concern flooded our school as we confronted bullying, female aggression, and even a lockdown perpetuated by an aggressive parent. Feeling as though we were living in an emotional war zone, teachers wondered what to do next. We tried to get used to teaching behind closed doors and dealing with indoor recess.

In the middle of this chaos, like a breath of fresh air, floated an unexplainable phenomenon—one that gave me hope that a safe, caring learning community is not only worth working for but may be within our grasp.

Out of the blue

Middle school students are known for their self-absorption and apparent inability to nurture the adults in their lives. Those of us who work with them come to expect this behavior. We accept it. We excuse it by saying that 10- to 15-year-olds are "in process" and will learn how to support those around them someday. In my class of sixth and seventh graders this week, the future made an unexpected appearance.

After reading my morning e-mail, I shared some sad news with my students. Their guidance counselor's father had died the night before. As we discussed this event, I reminded students that this teacher's mother had died only a few months ago. This time would be doubly difficult for their counselor.

Before I knew it, one of the students started making a large sympathy card for the teacher. The following message was written across the top of the card:

You Were There 4 Us
Now We Are Here for You

Classmates hovered around the card. Each student took a turn to write comforting words. Groups of students took the card around to the other middle school students. By the end of the day, the card, crammed with words of care and comfort, was carried to the school office so it could be delivered to their teacher. The card was testimony to a teacher who modeled care and support in a way that equipped these young people to give it back.

Modeling comfort

As I thought about this display of sensitivity, it became clear to me that educators are always being presented with opportunities to prepare students for caretaking roles, first by modeling and later by releasing them to take on those roles themselves. Such opportunities might take the form of service projects, or student leadership, or peer counseling opportunities.

In London, England, a wildly successful Peer Support Program *http://www.mentalhealth.org.uk/peer/peersupportbriefing.htm* identified positive outcomes for students who received training to be peer supporters. Those students

- Received training in communication skills.

- Learned to be open-minded and understanding listeners

- Developed different ways of communicating and learned the importance of confidentiality

- Developed the ability to deal with personal problems as well as support others.

- Learned from other peer supporters

- Helped others be more assertive

- Felt that becoming peer supporters made them feel more responsible

- Felt increased confidence.

As we seek to educate the whole child, service projects, student leadership, and peer counseling opportunities can become a powerful training ground. Through such opportunities, we can nurture young people who may one day, in a moment of need, take on the role of "peer comforter"—and everyone will wonder where that ability to rise to the occasion came from!

Additional Resouces

Peer Support Foundation
http://electricity.net.au/

This educational organization is committed to improving the quality of life for school students through peer group influence.

National Youth Service Day
http://www.ysa.org/nysd/index.cfm

This Web site shares how young people can be empowered by their ongoing contributions to their communities and mobilize their energy, commitment, and idealism through sustainable service.

Youth Service America
http://www.ysa.org/

Award service programs recognize and honor young people for their dedication to volunteer service.

Peer Resources
http://www.mentors.ca/peer.html

This site offers links to and descriptions of peer associations, services, and programs.

2.
Your Students: No Two Are Alike

When you watch Michael Jordan perform unforgettable maneuvers on the basketball court or listen to Celine Dion belt out one of her moving ballads, do you ever wonder how they did in school? I do. I wonder if they ever failed a math test or struggled to make sense of a Shakespearean sonnet. I wonder if their peers looked up to them. I wonder if their teachers had any idea of the world-class talents they would become.

I also wonder if I am too focused on meeting curriculum standards to notice in my own classroom a budding George Lucas, Maya Angelou, or Bill Gates. Would I recognize their talents if they showed up in ways other than what education theorist Howard Gardner calls "schoolhouse giftedness," or the more traditional linguistic and logical thinking?

Leaving no student behind

Those questions have led me to take a different approach during the first weeks of school. Others might condemn my approach as a frivolous use of precious class time, but I persist in putting aside the seemingly pressing issues of curriculum for a while. Instead, my students concentrate on creating their own learning profiles. The learning profile document (more specifics about this later) identifies and celebrates the eight intelligences identified by Howard Gardner. The function of the learning profile is twofold: to give me a bird's-eye view of the strengths and weaknesses of my new students, and to provide my students with some self-knowledge that will help them meet their learning potential.

Each year I am amazed at the wealth of unconventional information I gain from this activity. I encounter students who appear to live dual lives—they struggle during school hours but excel outside of school, demonstrating remarkable abilities in tap dancing, computer programming, hockey, or choral speech.

Knowing that students who are labeled learning disabled are frequently very creative in other ways, better than average at visual-spatial tasks, or talented in mechanical, musical, or athletic pursuits motivates me to seek out alternative ways of delivering my curriculum. I am often able to figure out approaches to my curriculum that will take advantage of their many and varied strengths.

Creating a learner profile

During the beginning days of school, I introduce two learning inventories to my students:

Multiple Intelligences Survey. First, I have them complete the Mutliple Intelligences Survey *http://www.ldrc.ca/projects/ miinventory/miinventory.php.* This survey identifies which of the eight intelligences—math-logic, verbal-linguistic, spatial, bodily-kinesthetic, musical, intrapersonal, interpersonal, and naturalistic—have the strongest influence on each student's ability to learn *http://www.ez2bsaved.com/Multiple_Intelligences/index-mi.htm#Diagram.* Although learners demonstrate elements of each of the eight intelligences, the survey helps identify several intelligences as dominant.

Learning-Style Preference Questionnaire. Are students orderly, reserved, cautious, or good at on-the-spot problem solving? Do they thrive when they can work with things that can be handled, taken apart, and put together again, or do they prefer working with things that directly and practically help people's lives? The Learning-Style Preference Questionnaire *http://lookingahead.heinle.com/filing/l-styles.htm* sheds light on many less conventional characteristics that contribute to an individual's success in learning.

After administering those two inventories, I introduce activities to help students internalize *what* they have learned about *how* they learn. For example:

- Students use data collected from the learning-style questionnaire to create their own Learning Styles Pie Chart.

- Arrange students into eight groups. Assign a different intelligence to each group. Students in each group research the assigned intelligence and create a poster or mural to help explain it to their classmates.

- Provide each student with a legal-size file folder. Have students create on the cover of the folder a collage comprised of pictures from magazines and other sources as well as their own art; each image should represent something the student discovered about himself or herself from the MI activities or questionnaires. We file those activities, students' goal sheets, and examples of student work in the folders. All this work can be used as a reference point during parent conferences.

- Provide students with a drawing of a large head. Have students divide the skull area into approximate areas represented by different intelligences. Label each section and add pictures, illustrations, or key words to represent each intelligence.

- Challenge students to devise ways they can stretch beyond their natural talents and interests; have them use one of their lowest multiple intelligences to complete a project.

During the balance of the school year, I remind myself from time to time of the activities we did in the first two weeks of school. Letting those learning profiles sit on a shelf was never my intent. The power of those tools is only unleashed when their contents are pondered, referred to, and applied to the curriculum throughout the year in the form of lessons.

Additional Resources

Little Geniuses
http://www.thomasarmstrong.com/articles/geniuses.htm

Psychologist Thomas Armstrong reminds us that giftedness comes in many forms.

Learning Styles and the Multiple Intelligences
http://www.ldpride.net/learningstyles.MI.htm

Teaching Style Inventory
http://www.indstate.edu/ctl/styles/tstyle.html

Teachers have learning styles too. Find out what yours is.

Learner Style Strategies Database
http://muskingum.edu/~cal/database/inventory.html

Celebrate Students' Abilities

In *Little Geniuses,* psychologist Thomas Armstrong celebrates more than three dozen unconventional talents that are worth developing and celebrating in children. Those talents include:

—Adventuresomeness	—Leadership abilities	—Persistence
—Common sense	—Manual dexterity	—Self-discipline
—Compassion	—Moral character	—Sense of humor
—Inquiring mind	—Patience	—Social savvy

3.
Curious to the Core

As a teacher of gifted and talented students, I spend my days surrounded by learners who excel at being curious. Their conversations are peppered with statements or questions:

> *I've got an idea ...*
> *Do you know ...?*
> *I'd like to find out ...*
> *What would happen if ...?*
> *Where can I find ...?*
> *Can we do an extra question?*

It's no wonder that this steady stream of inquiry can set some of these youngsters up for ridicule among their peers. Not everyone has an unquenchable thirst to know, and many students misinterpret such questioning banter as "brown-nosing" or bragging.

Teaching curious students has been a comfortable transition for me. One of the reasons I feel so at home is because of my own overactive curiosity concerning learning reform. I understand what it is like to have a mind that often operates in overdrive. As an educator, I am constantly on the lookout for methods that push the boundaries of conventional thought. The same type of questioning behavior exhibited by my students has fueled many of my own classroom initiatives.

Watching the resistance that my curious students encounter from their peers when they share ideas and questions might shed some light on why it can be difficult for teaching colleagues to celebrate one another's successes or willingly discuss learning reform.

Recognizing curious people

I have noticed that curious people share many similarities. They

- Love to share their *every* discovery
- Delight in making the impossible possible
- Thrive in problem-solving situations
- Often think with their mouths
- Are rarely satisfied with status quo answers and love the unusual
- Are in a hurry to meet their goals

- Seem to reach a level of success that threatens their peers
- Can exhaust themselves and other people with their questions and their desire to change and grow
- Can exhibit an intellectual arrogance that alienates themselves from their peers.

None of us is as smart as all of us

The traits above, if understood, might provide clues concerning how a diverse group of people can work together and support one another. Even my students have talked about and come up with strategies to help them relate to their peers—strategies such as the following:

Stop

- Be selective: Don't share every single thought and idea that comes into your mind. Others have valuable ideas to share too.
- People accept change at different speeds. Value the cautious as well as the curious.

Look

- Before you comment in a group, pause to see if one of your less impulsive peers has something to say.
- In your zeal, you may give the impression of being a know-it-all.

Listen

- There is an element of truth and wisdom within many ideas, even those with which you disagree.
- Listen for the underlying message in what others say. Their insecurities and need to be recognized may have a lot to do with their resistance to change.
- Pay attention to the unspoken message you are communicating.

Film director Sidney Pollack has some sound advice for educators who desire to unite the curious and the cautious so that educating young people can be completed: "...the more willing you seem to be to let people participate, the less need they have to force participation. It's the threat of being left out that exacerbates their ego problems and creates clashes."

Additional Resources

Characteristics of Various Areas of Giftedness
http://www.nagc.org/NSBA/chartcharacter.PDF

Many of these traits are exhibited by the "movers and shakers" of the teaching profession.

Nurturing Social-Emotional Development of Gifted Children
http://ericec.org/digests/e527.html

This article by James Webb documents potential problems that may be encountered when working with gifted learners.

The Secrets of Great Groups
http://www.pfdf.org/leaderbooks/121/winter97/bennis.html

Yes, a diverse group of people can work together. Leadership expert Warren Bennis explains why it is important and how it can happen.

Innovation Means Relying on Everyone's Creativity
http://www.pfdf.org/leaderbooks/121/spring2001/wheatley.html

Author Margaret Wheatley emphasizes the importance of staff collaboration and warns that uninvolved colleagues will "show up as resistors and saboteurs."

4.
Student Disinterest: Is it Curable?

Disinterested students are easy to spot! They meander into class, drop their books, and slide into semi-reclining positions at their desks. Indifference is written all over their faces—and all over the work they do.

Meanwhile, teachers scratch their heads and huddle together, trying to make sense of the lack of pride and drive those students show. We wonder if motivation can be taught, and we speculate on whether inspiring students is really part of our jobs.

All of us secretly hope that a tonic will be discovered to fix what ails those students; and we pray (outside of school, of course) that the disease is not contagious.

Helping students get "unstuck"

Students check out of the learning process for a variety of reasons —including poor self-esteem, being under- or over-challenged by the curriculum, turmoil at home, boredom, or illness. Most educators, however, are always seeking concrete ways to re-engage those disinterested students in the learning process. Following are some fresh ideas and words of wisdom I've gathered from my colleagues on the MiddleWeb Listserv *http://www.middleweb.com/mw/aaChat.html.*

Turn their natural inclinations into strength

- Work with what you've got. Middle schoolers flourish in herds—it's the nature of the beast. Group projects and an abundance of lunch-hour and after-school clubs will meet those students' need to be part of a group.

- Create projects that tap into their innate desire to make a difference in their world. Check out a few of the many Service Learning Web Resources available *http://www.goodcharacter. com/SERVICE/webresources.html* or connect learning themes to such social justice topics as famine, child labor, and children's rights.

- This generation loves to interact. Capitalize on that by integrating instant messaging (MSN) and online bulletin boards into your assignments. They'll be so busy writing that they won't even realize they're learning!

Actively Engage Students

- Enlist students' opinions whenever possible. Involve them in creating assignment rubrics. Frequently seek their feedback concerning what is happening in your classroom.

- Provide plenty of opportunities for student choice in the way they learn and in the ways they are allowed to demonstrate what they know. That will encourage them to take more ownership of their learning. Acquaint yourself with Howard Gardner's work in multiple intelligences, and be open to project work that goes beyond the traditional.

Reward Them

- Create a bulletin board headlined "Great Moments in Room 32." If you see a student doing something thoughtful or kind, write it down on an index card and hang it up on the board.

- Create a bulletin board that shouts "Stupendous Students." Let students choose the work they are most proud of to display.

Make Sure Structures Are in Place

- Communicate clear, reachable expectations. Routinely provide benchmarks and rubrics at the beginning of an assignment so students know what they have to do to achieve.

- Do whatever you have to do to help students meet your learning expectations for them. If reading 100 minutes a week at home is a turn-off for a disinterested student, start with 15 minutes and work up gradually. Students will be encouraged to make an effort if they know you are willing to work with them.

Meet Their Emotional Needs

- Consider publishing student work online. Nothing seems to motivate students quite as much as knowing their work will have an extended audience.

- Encourage administrators to make a special effort to work with troublesome students. They can offer extra love and support, a sincere "How are you doing?" in the morning, an extra hug when they need a time out, maybe even a trip to McDonald's at the end of a successful week.

- Ensure that learning is meaningful to the student. Whenever possible, make connections between the curriculum and their lives. Doing so will enhance their interest and make the learning (and teaching) easier.

- Teacher energy and enthusiasm can be significant to getting disinterested students engaged in learning. Nothing is quite as captivating as a teacher who is constantly on the brink of new learning discoveries—students can't help being enticed to jump on board for the learning ride ahead!

Additional Resources

What Students Need in the Restructured High School
http://www.edweek.org/ew/ewstory.cfm?slug=07hoffman.h22

What to do when you and your students have different agendas.

The Art and Craft of Motivating Students
http://www.successoriesonline.com/mmatters/html/edu_fall02/i_o_m.html

Dianne Walker explains how control, competency, and connection go a long way to help engage students in learning.

Motivating Students
http://www.hcc.hawaii.edu/intranet/committees/FacDevCom/guidebk/teachtip/motiv.htm

Barbara Gross Davis offers some practical tips.

5.
Students Reach for the "Skylights" of Learning

There are one-story intellects, two-story intellects, and three-story intellects with skylights. All fact collectors who have no aim beyond their facts are one-story men. Two-story men compare, reason, and generalize, using the labor of fact collectors as their own. Three-story men idealize, imagine, predict—their best illumination comes from above the skylight. —Oliver Wendell Holmes

As we have endeavored to catch a glimpse of the "skylights" of learning that Holmes refers to, we—the students in Mrs. Dyck's class—have also spent time in the second story, the first story, and sometimes even the basement!

Yes, we, like all learners, must spend some time in the basement. Doing math rewrites, reworking assignments, keeping track of notes, and sometimes dealing with behavioral issues, such as bullying *http://www. bullying.org/*—those are a few of the things we do in the basement. It can be kind of dark and discouraging down there, but Mrs. Dyck often comes down with a bright searchlight to remind us that we don't have to stay down there for long. She tells us that it is important to realize that this is the foundation of the building. Without a foundation of good work habits and redone assignments, our building would not stay up for long. A weak foundation definitely wouldn't support our upper-story thinking efforts. We have also learned that there are no shortcuts in the basement, no matter how slow and unproductive the time might seem.

Our first-story experiences are made up of quizzes, tests, and review activities *http://www.quia.com/jg/124023.html*. We have discovered that if we put in the time, life on the first story can be quite pleasant. There we experience success; we even feel like we know a lot. Mrs. Dyck doesn't seem to be satisfied with life on the first story, though. Using the facts that we've learned seems to be more important to her than just collecting those facts. She is always taking the information that we've gathered on the first story and asking us to follow her up "those slippery, hazy stairs" to the next story above us.

Time on the first story is really never wasted, Mrs. Dyck reminds us, because without it we wouldn't have the courage or even the ability to move up to those higher stories.

On to the second story—and the third

We have to admit that it's a bit of an adventure up here on the second story. We've discovered that it isn't enough to just spit out those facts that we gathered on the first level. As a matter of fact, to do that seems rather boring. Instead of just filling in blanks and answering questions with pat answers, we get to use such tools as fishbone diagrams *http://www.skymark. com/resources/tools/cause.asp*, Venn diagrams *http://home.earthlink.net/~tsdobbs/go/ goperry.jpg*, and flowcharts *http://www.skymark.com/resources/tools/flowchart.asp* to transport our facts to another level of understanding. We use a variety of other graphic organizers for this purpose too *http://home.earthlink.net/~tsdobbs/ Graphic_Organizers/graphic_organizers.html*.

If life on the second story is an adventure, life on the third story provides a quick look at the future. Some of us haven't been to the third story yet. We hear you there only after spending a lot of time roaming around on the second floor. The third floor is a place where our imaginations take off and we are free to envision a better future or experience a defining moment in our learning. The thing about the third story is that it isn't somewhere you just camp out. You will need to revisit all the other stories for the opportunity to spend time on the third story. You will catch only a glimpse of the third story after spending lots of time on the lower stories.

See an example of our third story writing and thinking *http://www. occdsb.on.ca/~proj1615/leaders/custom4.html*. In this project, called "I'm Leading, Is Anybody Following?" we examined various leaders throughout history in light of the seven characteristics of a good leader.

See another sample of upper-level thinking *http://www.masters.ab.ca/bdyck/ Leader/Leaderthree/Democracy%20Two.jpg*. In this activity, we demonstrated our abilities to synthesize, a third story learning skill, by translating an abstract idea, such as democracy, into a concrete model.

The reason there are skylights on the third level is because once you get there, you realize that there are fourth, fifth, sixth, or more stories! The sky is the limit! Mrs. Dyck says that those are the places of Profound Learning. She says learning at those levels isn't always about math, science, or social studies. Sometimes the learning there is about believing in your ability to learn or using a skill that you learned in a lower level to make a life-changing decision.

Signed,
Along for the Climb
(Mrs. Dyck's Grade 6 Class)

6.
Surprised By Reading:
Confessions of a Math Teacher

I've just about finished reading *From the Mixed-Up Files of Mrs. Basil E. Frankweiler* (*http://www.peak.org/~bonwritr/BOOK_mixedupfiles.htm*) to my grade six students. I admit this rather sheepishly because I am not a language arts teacher—I teach math.

The truth is, I really miss the bonding experience that goes with reading aloud to students. That's why I've been reading to them in homeroom or whenever we can grab a few minutes. They beg me to read. They frequently ask me what we will read next.

I must admit I have been a little surprised by my students' enthusiasm. At first, I thought their interest was related to being allowed to "play hooky" from math. Then one day, when I happened to look up from my reading, I realized that 25 pairs of eyes were glued to me. All ears were listening with rapt anticipation. Another give-away about their interest was the questions and comments fired my way as I passed students in the hall:

Are you reading to us today?

We haven't been read to in class for a long time. I love being read to.

I've been thinking about the book. If Claudia and Jamie spent $3.00 a day at the museum, wouldn't they have run out of money?

When was that book written? I figure it had to be a long time ago, since a newspaper only cost 10 cents.

What is it about being read to?

I wanted to learn more about this phenomenon (to me, anyway) I was observing; so one day, I asked my students point-blank why they enjoyed being read to so much. They told me:

When you get older, no one ever reads to you in school.

I love your voice. It helps me picture what's going on in the story, and I don't have to struggle with figuring the words out.

It's so relaxing. It helps me settle down so that I can work later.

I asked my colleagues if they were reading aloud to their students. I learned that few teachers felt they could take the time, even though they wished they could.

One teacher told me that the University of Oxford makes a practice of organizing "reading salons"—where professors read aloud scholarly works to their students. It appears that, in the midst of their emphasis on teaching and research, even this prestigious university recognizes the value of reading aloud to students! It seems they recognize some of the many benefits reading aloud can bring. Reading aloud

- Engages listeners while developing background knowledge, increasing comprehension skills, and fostering critical thinking
- Models the use of reading strategies that aid in comprehension
- Exposes students to books beyond their reading level
- Expands a listener's vocabulary
- Stimulates the imagination.

The love of reading is caught, not taught

I've discovered that the books we read to our students can have a life that goes far beyond the classroom. Reading *The Mixed Up Files of Mrs. Basil E. Frankweiler* has unleashed a dream in one of my students. Because of her strong interest in this book, she and her mother are currently planning a trip to the Metropolitan Museum of Art, the setting for the book. She tells me the book started it all.

I knew I had hit on something the day one of my struggling, disinterested students shoved a scrap of paper and a pencil my way and said, "Will you write the name of the book and the author down, please? I want to read it on my own."

A few days later, while reading to the class, I looked up, and there she was, reading along with me. She had bought her own copy of the book! That must be what author Thomas Carlyle meant when he wrote, "The best effect of any book is that it excites the reader to self-activity."

Additional Resources

Read Alouds: Is It Worth It?
http://www.educationworld.com/a_curr/curr213.shtml

Education World explores the benefits of reading out loud to students.

Reading Aloud—Are Students Ever Too Old?
http://www.educationworld.com/a_curr/curr081.shtml

Read about teachers who are making time to read to students in the older grades.

StoryLine Online
http://www.bookpals.net/storyline/welcome.html

There's nothing quite as exciting as being read to by a famous person. This online streaming video program features famous actors reading children's books aloud.

7.
Each Student Is Someone's Special Child

Many of you will remember the day in April 1970 when moon-bound Apollo 13 astronaut Jack Swigert announced to the world, "Houston, we have a problem here!" With that statement, a routine trip to the moon suddenly became a life-threatening voyage. Ground controllers faced the grueling task of getting three American astronauts home alive. They managed to do so only because, as they said, "Failure wasn't an option."

I have thought of that incident many times as I parented my own children. I am hard-pressed to think of many examples of times when anyone other than my husband or me has shown that "failure is not an option" level of commitment to my children.

Did I ever show such commitment to my students in the first years of my teaching career? I'm sure I didn't. I was 22-years-old and keen to do the very best I could for my students, but I had no experience of going the extra mile for children whose learning or behavioral difficulties eluded me. Parenting changed that!

Teaching mom to mom

I returned to the classroom after raising five children. I had spent a decade observing how educators had met—and not met—the learning and behavioral needs of my kids. Rigid pedagogy and a reluctance to go the extra mile to meet learning and behavioral needs often perplexed me. My newfound perspective amounted to a teaching epiphany! It would have a profound impact on how I would teach. I vowed to treat my students as I would want my own children treated. I would treat them as someone's special child, a child for whom failure was not an option.

Being a parent was the best preparation I ever had for the classroom. As I teach today, I try to keep fresh in my mind parenting memories:

- The morning chaos that led me to forget to sign an important notice for one of my children
- The nights I was dead tired and unable to help my children prepare for a test
- The effort I put into figuring out projects that had scant or indecipherable instructions
- My guilt when my child failed a test

- How a demanding home reading program had the potential to do me in.

Those memories provide insight for me into the homes my students come from. It's easier to extend grace to my students and parents when I remember the demands of parenting, when I consider how my students' parents are often doing the best they can do.

As a parent, you become a proficient cheerleader, problem solver, and organizer of the disorganized. Seeing how my own children needed step-by-step guidance through large learning projects and test preparation helped me recognize that my students at school would benefit from that same level of support. I try to consider the students' parents as I teach. Clear assignment expectations, frequent home-school communication, and step-by-step writing templates have become routine classroom practices for me. All classroom practices are designed to help students succeed.

Working with large groups of active children for hours at a time can stretch anybody's energy and patience. When under stress, it is so easy for any teacher to holler or speak in a demeaning manner. I try to keep in mind that I am speaking to children who matter a great deal to their parents. That helps me bite my tongue or, in other cases, apologize for thoughtless words. I try to keep in mind that my own children recall many of the positive comments their teachers made—even ten years after the fact! That helps me focus on regularly affirming my students.

Children come in all shapes and sizes. So do their learning styles. With that knowledge, I often take students aside to find an approach that will meet their particular learning needs. I always try to consider how grateful I would be if a teacher made that effort on behalf of my child. I always try to think of that Houston ground crew for whom failure was not an option.

Additional Resources

Failure Is Not an Option
http://www.historychannel.com/option/

Gain a better understanding about Gene Kranz, the flight director who didn't give up on the Apollo 13 astronauts.

Is That Penguin Stuffed or Real?
http://www.pdkintl.org/kappan/k_v78/k9612oha..htm

Education writer Susan Ohanian reflects that teaching children is not a project for the impatient.

8.
Service Projects Help Students Find Their Voices

I've discovered there is a powerful, untapped resource simmering within my school walls. It's not a new brand of teacher, a hotshot program, or a new learning initiative. This potent resource smolders deep within the very students I teach. Most of the time I miss it, distracted by the academic and behavioral irritations that plague my daily involvement with students. I get a hint of it during those rare inspirational moments when a service challenge is put before them. A recent service learning project reminded me how our students' youthful enthusiasm, idealism, and energy can move mountains.

Working for a common goal

The project began with a simple assembly where a challenge was presented. Students were introduced to a local organization called The Cave. The Cave serves the needs of troubled young people in our community who, for a variety of reasons, find themselves without a home or some of life's most basic amenities. Students in the school were presented with the idea of supporting The Cave's efforts to keep kids off the streets.

The project—which we called Street Cents—challenged students throughout the school to join forces to collect money for The Cave. For five consecutive days students brought in money from home. Teachers made hurried trips to the bank to convert hundreds of dollars into 50-penny rolls *http://www.masters.ab.ca/bdyck/Street/Roll/index.html*. We chose to convert the money to pennies because of the visual impact a very large collection of pennies might have on our students.

Money came in right up until the last moment, as students scrounged around in their lockers, looking for an extra penny or quarter to add to their class's collection.

The week culminated in another assembly on Friday—"Street Cents Day." At that assembly, each class lined up in the gym with its collection of penny rolls at the head of the line. Line leaders passed penny rolls down their lines so each student in the class could start forming part of the penny line. As upbeat music filled the air, penny rolls were unwrapped, and classmates worked shoulder to shoulder to form lines of pennies *http://www.masters.ab.ca/bdyck/Street/Student/index.html*. One of our more spirited teachers announced in DJ style the penny progress as each class line of pennies was formed and the class that collected the most pennies was determined.

At the end we all stood back, amazed, at the view before us. Forty-five thousand pennies were lined up side by side on the floor, creating a visual image that they all will carry with them for the rest of their lives! *http://www. masters.ab.ca/bdyck/Street/Line2/index.html.*

Almost as surprising was the number of students who stuck around for the clean up! Sweeping up 45,000 pennies was no small job *http://www. masters.ab.ca/bdyck/Street/Sweep/index.html,* and we had volunteers who not only swept but searched the floor for wayward pennies. Many even willingly offered to help re-roll the pennies so they could be taken back to the bank.

Tapping into what motivates

The Street Cents project had taken what our students bring to school every day—their enthusiasm, energy, and desire to make a difference—and used it in a productive way. I wonder what would happen if we viewed these service challenges as part of our students' education instead of an *addition* to it? Could the same meaningful, life-changing learning happen on a daily basis if we connected our students' passion to our program? If so, then making a difference could become the fuel that drives our daily curriculum instead of just a seasonal activity.

Additional Resources

Giving Teens Good Press
http://www.riverdeep.net/current/2000/12/121300_magazines.jhtml

Read about teens who are changing their world.

Service Learning in Action Across the Grades
http://www.educationworld.com/a_curr/curr187.shtml

An *Education World* article explains ways that service projects enhance classroom programs.

A Different Kind of Education
http://riverdeep.net/current/2000/10/100600_kid.jhtml

There's much more to learning than the 3 R's.

Make a Difference Day
http://usaweekend.com/diffday/index.html

A unique program that inspires and rewards volunteers.

Do Something

http://www.dosomething.org/

A nationwide network of young people who take action to change the world around them.

Getting Kids to "Do Something."

http://www.educationworld.com/a_curr/curr385.shtml

An *Education World* article about the Do Something Program.

Earth Inc.—A Service-Learning Lesson Plan

http://www.educationworld.com/a_lesson/lesson154.shtml

An *Education World* article focuses on the Social Studies Education Consortium, which offers a template for a model service project.

Is Community Service a Waste of Time?

http://www.educationworld.com/a_curr/curr188.shtml

Education World talks to the experts about what it takes to create a real service learning project—if that's possible.

Community Service: Opportunity or Exploitation?

http://www.educationworld.com/a_curr/curr037.shtml

What about mandatory community service programs in schools? Are they a wonderful opportunity or are they "slave labor" for students?

9.
Looking at Your Students in the Future Tense

You know, Giono said to me, there are also times in life when a person has to rush off in pursuit of hopefulness.
— Norma L. Goodrich

After a week of tripping over backpacks in the hall, chasing down students for assignments, and dealing with yet another bullying incident, I wondered if there might be an easier way to earn a living. Even the most vigilant educator needs an occasional reminder that his or her efforts with students are contributing to future successes, especially when the present seems void of any evidence that students are embracing our efforts.

Last night, I got a timely reminder at an Arts Celebration Night at our K-12 school. Here, I was treated to a glimpse of the young people my former students are becoming. Having taught many of these high school students at one time or another, I found it especially rewarding to see former students profiled in such a positive way, doing things that three or four years ago my colleagues and I would not have thought possible.

My students?

One of my former students, William, was busy helping with the sound system. When I taught William I was lucky to have him finish an assignment, let alone contribute to such an important element of a concert. Come to think of it though, William always shone when given the opportunity to work with his hands. In my mind's eye, I remember being able to count on William to vacuum a mess up in my class or mop a spill in the hallway. Today, he was feeling pretty important as he ran around looking for sound cords after school.

Then there was Anita, a quiet, insecure girl who was in my class several years ago. Anita struggled with low self-esteem. Tonight, however, I saw a new and confident Anita emerge as she danced across the stage in a dramatic lead role. Somewhere between grade six and today, Anita had found a way to express what was going on inside of her and convert her insecurities into creativity.

Most surprising to me was Jerry. A few years ago Jerry was an introverted boy with few friends. His monotone voice made everyone think Jerry was a little slow and uninteresting. When he got up to sing a ballad

last night, I wondered where this incredible voice had come from and
wondered how his talent had passed me by three years ago.

Part of a bigger picture

In the back of the darkened gym, sandwiched between my middle
school colleagues, I kept thinking about a number of other performers,
who in my memory were once nervous, troublesome, or sad grade six
students. Some probably still are, but for one special night, they showed the
audience their potential and reminded me that I am an important link in a
long continuum of educators teaching young people who are still "works in
progress." From where I sat, my job now looked pretty good!

Additional Resources

What Does It Mean To Be Thirteen?
http://www.nmsa.org/moya/new2002/pk_related_itmean.html

Chris Stevenson, a middle school teacher and principal, compares the
world of a 13-year-old child—past and present.

Understanding and Appreciating the Wonder Years
http://www.nmsa.org/moya/new2002/pk_related_understanding.html

John Lounsbury sheds some light on the nature of the middle school
student.

Reflections From a Teacher's Heart
http://www.middleweb.com/puckett.html

David Puckett's insightful book of poems describes the highs and lows
of teaching in the middle grades.

III. Teachers

I have come to a frightening conclusion.
I am the decisive element in the classroom.
It is my personal approach that creates the climate.
It is my daily mood that makes the weather.
As a teacher I possess tremendous power to make a child's life
*   miserable or joyous.*
I can be a tool of torture or an instrument of inspiration.
I can humiliate or humor, hurt or heal.
In all situations, it is my response that decides whether a crisis
*   will be escalated or de-escalated,*
*   and a child humanized or de-humanized.*

— Haim Ginott

1.
American Teachers: A Strength Exposed

We have gained new heroes ... those who battled their own fears to keep children calm and safe—America's teachers.
— President George W. Bush
Address to the Nation,
November 8, 2001

My role as an educator is multifaceted. In addition to teaching, I am responsible for gathering and saving the daily e-mail postings from MiddleWeb listserv discussions so that they can be posted in an easy-to-read format for readers. I collect and preserve the thoughts, feelings, observations, and struggles of some of the savviest educators found in our profession.

Today I find myself poring through the archives from the week surrounding September 11, 2001. It is my own personal way of remembering the events of that day. I am moved by what I read, for before my eyes I see brief listserv postings suddenly transformed from random e-mails to meaningful historical documents that expose the strength and courage of the educators who walked the nation's children through the initial shock of the September 11th terrorist attacks on America.

The first teacher posting of that day sounded like a quiet voice crying in the wilderness: *My class has just spent the last period watching ABC news. This is so devastating; how do we explain this terrorism to our children?*

This cry for help seemed to jolt educators into response mode. A rash of e-mails began to flood in. A teacher at a Department of Defense School in Germany described the chaos and fear around her:

Thank God our children are already home. We are now locked in on our local bases. No one can be out except essential personnel. Our students are all too aware of the implications for us. They are expecting problems here in Europe directed at us. Explaining this is not easy, not totally possible... We find that explaining is not so much necessary as letting the students talk about how they feel and how this makes them feel. I will also do some writing probably through the journals and let them talk it out in their discussion groups.

Many teachers spoke of their frustrations and emotions:

Our district superintendent has put the kibosh on conversation for today at school.

I get the feeling that students are amazed that something "this bad" can happen in the United States. ... The only time I have seen the children completely fearful or upset is when a teacher has made a speculative remark about the responsible parties, repercussions of this action, or possible future actions in the presence of children. I urge you to remember that children's ears hear even when the conversation is not directed towards them.

Unfortunately the cancellation of the football game tonight seemed to be more important to some of the kids. ... How can I best explain to them how irrelevant the game is?

One issue we ran into today was racial slurs being made about people of Arab descent. Our hope is that our students don't judge people based on their race.

I was humbled again as I drove home seeing so many moms and dads picking their kids up at school and walking home together as a family, holding hands. It made me cry. It made me feel like the very fabric of my world was under attack by someone.

The recent terrorist acts in New York and Washington have left me reeling. ... I believe New York City mayor, Rudy Giuliani, said it best: "Today, everyone is a New Yorker!"

Teachers had to put their own fears aside so that they could attend to the fears of their students and parents:

I am truly horrified and not sure how we will handle things at school tomorrow.

We also dealt with upset, worried, perplexed students. Teachers struggled to carry on their lessons in spite of sick feelings in their stomachs and an awareness that something very precious had just died. We were very cognizant that teachers would be the first adults these children would be looking to for comfort and answers, and we handled that trust with compassion and honesty.

I know it is going to be chaotic, and the students will be frightened since we [in Europe] are "on the front lines" all the time the way it is. We will spend seminar talking about this and allowing the students to share their fears and feelings. Many have family and friends near where the hot spots were today as they are not that far from military bases. If we go to war, my students' parents will be some of the first to go. This is terrifying for all of us.

Here in the metro Washington, D.C., area it looks like a surreal painting. Some of our students have parents who work in or near the Pentagon. The National Institutes of Health is across the street from the Navy Medical Center. There are armed guards all over the place.

There was a rush of parents at one point because a radio announcer caused panic.

Virtual friendships are no different from any other. It wasn't long before listserv members were asking about the whereabouts of one of our New York City listserv colleagues.

I just want to know if Naomi is okay. Do we have any other listserv members in New York City?

Driving home listening to NPR today, I was doubly anxious to get home—to see my family, and to check in with you all. I too was thinking of Naomi.

All of us breathed a sigh of relief when we finally heard from Naomi:

It was a rough day, but we made it. I had to walk across the bridge into Manhattan to get home, since they weren't letting cars in. Now we have to deal with the aftermath. It has been scary. I suppose that if we don't have world peace—we don't have any peace. —Naomi

I am so thankful that all our NYC friends have messaged us. Thank you so much. Yesterday I couldn't bear to even e-mail the list to ask about Naomi. I was overwhelmed with sadness. So I am reminded to be thankful for every minute and for the priceless things in my life—my family and friends, and I count you guys among my dearest cyber friends.

One teacher shared examples of middle school students at their best:

With all the shock and questions and all, two moments stood out for me at the school. One was of one ninth grade boy reaching over to stroke the hair and cheek of another ninth grade boy who was upset and had his head down on his desk. Another was of one eighth grade girl who just minutes before in the classroom had piercingly asked, "Why can't we all be at peace?" [Now she was] looking over the roof of the school at the moon between the trees and saying, "How beautiful it is!"

What will the afterimage of 9/11 be for our students? What will they remember about these chaotic days with us? Like President Bush, I believe that their afterimages will include the teachers who created order out of chaos, assurance out of fear, and protection from perceived danger.

We must not show our children panic or lack of control. They must feel confident in us and that we will protect them and keep them from harm. Whether or not we can, in reality, keep them from a terrorist attack is not the point. They need the reassurance and belief that we can.

Additional Resource

MiddleWeb Listserv
   http://www.middleweb.com/

2.
Asleep on the Job

Some of my colleagues at school claim that I am one brick short of a load. Each spring, they remind me of this as they observe me organizing my annual Grade Six Sleepover. I have to admit that as Sleepover day approaches, I too wonder whether this event represents a moment of insanity on my part. Organizing parent supervisors, calling breakfast crews, selecting menus, packing sleeping bags, and anticipating a night of nominal sleep usually causes me to question whether just having a picnic would be easier. All my doubts disappear around the time the first student arrives—early!

It happened again this year. Hardly able to contain his excitement, Jake turned up one hour early. Grateful for another pair of hands, I put Jake to work setting up tables for our midnight snack and carrying candles and a tape deck down into the darkest part of the basement. Swearing Jake to secrecy, I share what will happen in this creepy cellar later in the evening. His brown eyes shine because now he is part of the conspiracy.

Creating an experience like this for my grade six students is rather uncharacteristic for me. A core teacher in a testing year finds it so easy to have a serious plan in place at all times. Having my students' scores published in the newspaper each fall isn't often far from my mind. That night, however, the Grade Six Sleepover blurs my preoccupation with scores as we walk to the neighborhood ice cream shop or have a water fight outside the school. (To the kids' surprise, I plant myself on the school roof and throw pails of water on their heads! I have to admit it *is* kind of satisfying!) Standards and assessment are far from my mind as we

- Play Sardines (reverse Hide-and-Go-Seek) in the dark inside the school
- Creep down into the deepest, darkest corner of the furnace room—only candles lighting our way—for a motivational, end-of-the-year send-off story
- Watch *Remember the Titans* in the gym
- Sleep in the school—boys and girls are separated, in case you're wondering
- Enjoy a wonderful parent-made breakfast.

We laugh, we run—even this 48-year-old body runs—and we joke. Parents chitchat, hold candles in the dark while I read to their kids, help me herd students from activity to activity, and cook breakfast. The children appear to be amazed that I can tear around like a water maniac, participate in spooky experiences, show them my tacky pajamas, and hang out on the floor watching movies. Actually, it kind of surprises me too—because so much of my life is spent in the serious realm.

Year after year, the kids and parents tell me that the Sleepover is the one thing they remember about their grade six year. If that is so, perhaps I need to inject some of this craziness into my classroom more frequently. What long-term learning might occur if I infused my teaching with the unexpected, the humorous, and the power of relationships?

Additional Resources
Emotions and Learning
http://edservices.aea7.k12.ia.us/edtech/classroom/brain/emotion.html

This practical Web page examines how feelings of pleasure, anger, or frustration can support or hinder the learning process.

Teaching With Fun and Humor
http://www.etni.org.il/farside/humorme.htm

Jan Fall shares how fun and laughter in the classroom can enhance learning, boost student health, and reduce stress levels.

Humor in the Mathematics Classroom?
http://www.nade.net/documents/SCP94/SCP94.14.pdf

Chuck Nicewonder connects humor in the mathematics classroom with enhanced classroom climate and improved grades.

Ten Games for Classroom Fun
http://www.education-world.com/a_lesson/lesson169.shtml

This *Education World* site provides teachers with a variety of games to play with their students.

3.
Fragile in February

Have you ever noticed that teaching morale is cyclical? Each year we find ourselves smack in the middle of February, wondering where our September optimism went. An onslaught of unsettling events in February can make you wonder whether there is a conspiracy at work—one meant to perturb and discourage those of us who teach.

The new students I inherited after Christmas have made great progress in their behavior and their ability to focus. This week, however, they have reverted to their old ways. Today we finished our class by "dialoguing" about what went wrong this week. The students said they were tired, were discouraged by their teachers, and didn't much like the assignments that were coming their way. I didn't tell them that on that particular day, I felt much the same way as they did.

After school, I sat through a two-hour staff meeting that focused on the declining behavior in our school. This group of yawning, discouraged educators agreed that lack of respect and rotten attitudes students were showing had finally eroded their patience. The principal commented on the heaviness she sensed in our meeting. Our guidance counselor said he felt the room was heavy with fatigue.

It's strange, but the ambience of school is so different in September. Hope, enthusiasm, and vision for the future permeate every corner of the building. Teachers can't wait to implement ideas pondered over the summer. February, on the other hand, is screaming with reality checks —hopes that haven't materialized, problems that don't seem to have solutions, and a sense of feeling tired to the bone.

I wonder whether our students go through their own February crisis each year? They too begin each September with a sense of optimism, hoping new friendships and learning successes might make the new school year different for them. However, here they are in February failing some classes, bored in others, and drowning in the same old behavior issues. Hmm—just when I had decided that my students caused my February crisis, I need to ponder whether perhaps I've contributed to theirs! Perhaps a combination of the two makes for a stressful learning environment.

Parenting is kind of like that too. We experience intermittent Februarys. We hang in there mostly because we signed up for the long haul and because every so often a September experience reminds us of our child's potential.

I'll tell you what I do when I hit the wall of February; I intentionally remember past successes from my classroom. I try to recall

- The times I connected with a student with whom no one else could connect
- When the learning synergy between me and my students soared
- The ordinary lesson plan that became exceptional
- Those moments when the students became completely engaged in the learning moment
- The struggling learner that finally "got it"
- My own learning breakthroughs.

I've discovered that these recollections, a little rest and relaxation, and some thoughts about the spring that is on its way can help put these February lows in perspective. A little reflection on past successes can transport me from February to September in a flash!

Additional Resources

Catching Up With Our Bodies: Reflections on Teacher Burnout
http://www.education-world.com/a_curr/curr344.shtml

Another article about teaching in February.

Stress
http://teachers.net/gazette/FEB02/jones.html

Joy Jones explores why one-third of new teachers leave the teaching profession within five years.

Inspirational Teacher Stories
http://www.lessonplanspage.com/Inspiration.htm

Short on your own reasons for teaching? Take a look at these.

4.
Catching Up With Our Bodies:
Reflections on Teacher Burnout

In the deep jungles of Africa, a traveler was making a long trek. Natives had been engaged from a tribe to carry the loads. The first day they marched rapidly and went far. The traveler had high hopes of a speedy journey. But the second morning these jungle tribesmen refused to move. For some strange reason they just sat and rested. On inquiry as to the reason for this strange behavior, the traveler was informed that they had gone too fast the first day, and that they were now waiting for their souls to catch up with their bodies.

— Lettie Cowman

It happened again last February. Once again I found myself thinking about the profession that I've been a part of since I was 21 years of age. Back then, February had more to do with Valentine's Day, the upcoming school musical, and most importantly, my new husband. Over the years, I have noticed that February is a time when many educators start to question

- Why they chose this profession in the first place
- Why the line between personal and professional life is so unclear
- Why so many teachers are weary and cynical
- Whether it is possible to regain their previous zeal.

February is the time of year when teachers who have had one too many February experiences may choose to leave the profession.

In the past, I would silence those February questions by going to bed early for a few weeks, temporarily cutting back on the hours I spent at school, and cutting back my marking load. Within a few weeks, I'd be back in the saddle not only feeling better but also feeling rejuvenated for the last term of school.

I've been thinking about how it has become much more common to see teachers withdraw to refuel or even disappear from the profession altogether. Perhaps as a result, there seems to be a growing awareness within the teaching profession that overwork by teachers is, in the end, counterproductive to creating a healthy learning community. "Teachers who experience burnout are less sympathetic toward students, are less committed to and involved in their jobs, have a lower tolerance for classroom disruption, are less apt to prepare adequately for class, and are generally less productive," observed Kenneth Leithwood, professor and head of the Center for Leadership Development at the Ontario Institute for Studies in Education, University of Toronto.

This year it occurred to me that my little February regime was really a Band-Aid solution—a quick fix that temporarily solved the problem. Lettie Cowman's insightful tale caused me to consider whether each February my soul was actually trying to catch up with my body.

Like most educators, I spend most of my year thinking, breathing, and living school, so it was quite possible that this absorption had left my soul far behind! Fueled by that thought, I determined to use Stephen Covey's method of "beginning with the end in mind." *What would a teacher whose body and soul were in sync look like?* After talking with colleagues, and those outside our profession, I came up with a few benchmarks. An "in-sync" teacher, I've determined, might

- Take care of self and family first
- Reclaim time to think
- Put a little more life into self
- Leave paperwork at school
- Limit late hours at school
- Make a concentrated effort to think and talk and dream about family and interests.

It is interesting to note that in Lettie Cowman's story, we never find out how long it takes for the soul to catch up with the body. Maybe that's because it's the lessons we learn while waiting that are the most valuable.

Additional Resources

Total Teacher Wellness

http://www.speakwell.com/well/2000_fall/articles/total_teacher_wellness.html

In this article from *WELL*, the newsletter for wellness, Martin Collis, documents that Prozac use by teachers in Alberta, Canada, went up 30 percent in 1998. The Japanese even have a special phrase, *gakkyu kokai,* for the classroom collapse of teachers.

Is Teachers' Work Never Done?

http://radicalpedagogy.icaap.org/content/issue2_1/02Michelson.html

William Michelson, of the Sociology Department at the University of Toronto, examines teacher workload and the stress that results. This is a very thorough, thought-provoking piece of research.

Stress Busters for Teachers: Top Ways to Prevent Burnout
http://stressrelease.com/strssbus.html

Here are quick, practical ideas for educators who feel a stress attack coming.

Urban School Restructuring and Teacher Burnout
http://www.ericdigests.org/1992-4/urban.htm

Burnout—the reaction to prolonged high stress—commonly results in either withdrawing and caring less or working harder, often mechanically, to the point of exhaustion. This digest considers the impact of several components of school restructuring on burnout.

Teacher Stress and Burnout
http://interact.uoregon.edu/wrrc/Burnout.html

A vital key in coping with burnout is the realization that it is not something that happens only once in a lifetime. It appears again and again. Recognizing the symptoms is key to catching it before it catches you.

5.
Teaching With Heart

How do you revive a floundering classroom program? What causes a whole class of students to connect with one teacher and not with another? Those are two of the questions on my mind as I prepare for my newest teaching assignment—bringing order and synergy back into a sagging school program. For the next four weeks I will be working with a seventh-grade teacher to help her rework her program and repair the strained relationship with her students. As usual, I will look for any learning I can glean for myself along the way.

What makes an excellent teacher?

Why do some teachers bond with students and others have difficulty? Does it have a lot to do with the personality of the teacher? In most cases, I believe not. I believe that bonding with students is influenced by something more. I have witnessed fruitful student-teacher relationships in classrooms where I have considered the teachers in charge to be quiet or outgoing, funny or bland, energetic or placid. When I reflect on memorable educators from my past, I am struck by the lack of similarity among their teaching styles. Some lectured and some spoke very little, some were wildly imaginative and others approached their material in a very linear fashion; some were stuck on the rules while others believed in giving students a great deal of freedom.

But among the favorite teachers from my schooldays and all the terrific teachers I've observed since then, I *do* see some common characteristics. Even though I've long ago forgotten many of the facts imparted to me by the teachers from my past, I can still remember the feeling I had in their classes, my desire to do well, and the stories they told. I conclude that their teaching success had less to do with technique and a whole lot to do with a fresh, ongoing zeal for their subject as well as a consuming care and respect for their students. They were "teaching with heart."

Maintaining zeal for teaching

Teachers are "on deck" every day, 200 days a year. But it isn't always easy to get excited about the content we teach. That can be draining, especially when those we deliver our curriculum message to are focused on just about anything else but what we have to say.

Add to that an ongoing requirement to change with the times, the need for continuous improvement, and increased accountability and responsibility, and it is easy to see how a teacher might lose his or her passion for teaching. Keeping the zeal that first drew us to our craft requires that we take time to nurture our passion. It is difficult to share a stale message with enthusiasm. We need to be on a constant lookout for ways to re-ignite the interest that first attracted us to teaching. We can do that by

- Reading about our area of interest
- Attending professional development sessions
- Writing down our reflections and discoveries
- Hanging around with people who are innovative
- Talking with people who share the same passions we have.

Communicating to students that we care

I have become increasingly aware that emotions can affect the learning climate in my classroom. Students learn more effectively when they feel safe, cared for, and validated. Providing that type of environment is an important part of what teachers must do. We can accomplish that by

- Spending part of our class time getting to know our students' interests and thoughts
- Giving students eye contact and a smile
- Telling students about our lives and interests
- Taking time to make curriculum relevant to our students
- Focusing on important areas of contention and ignoring nonessential conflicts
- Bending the rules from time to time so the students know we are human
- Doing all we can to support our students' learning until they are mature or interested enough to take on some of those responsibilities themselves
- Speaking encouragement into our students' lives on a daily basis.

Many educators entered this profession thinking they could make a difference in their students' lives. For most of us, that was an act of the heart. My role over the next month will be to help a colleague revisit some of the things that attracted her to teaching in the first place—an exercise that will, no doubt, benefit both of us.

Additional Resources

Steps to Success in Being a Teacher
http://www.fariborz.com/onbeinga.htm

Great advice to keep teachers on track.

The Spirit of Teaching
http://www.middleweb.com/mw/msdiaries/01-02wklydiaries/EB14.html

Teacher Ellen Berg has been keeping a diary on MiddleWeb where she shares insights gained while teaching a challenging class.

Notes From a Teacher/Soldier in the Learning Revolution
http://www.middleweb.com/StdCtrdTchng.html

Educator Mari Clayton Glamser reflects on becoming more student-centered in her approach to teaching.

Asleep on the Job
http://www.educationworld.com/a_curr/curr349.shtml

More reflections on connecting with students.

Educators on the Edge
http://www.edweek.org/tm/tmstory.cfm?slug=07intro.h12

Read about five teachers who teach with heart.

Teacher Town, USA
http://www.edweek.org/tm/tmstory.cfm?slug=02town.h12

Emporia, Kansas, is a town that honors teachers who teach with heart.

6.
And We Shall Morph Again!

There is nothing like returning to a place that remains unchanged to find the ways in which you yourself have altered. —Nelson Mandela

September, and once again I find myself thinking back to my first year as a teacher. I can picture the dress I wore on the first day of school and even the faces of the students who were in my first class. Highlights from that year come to mind, along with the challenges that came amidst learning everything for the first time. Now, 25 years later, it occurs to me that I don't feel a whole lot different this September than I did that first September. Once again, I am starting a new teaching position, one that will require me to transform into yet another form of educator.

Morph—to be transformed

The ability to morph is one of the key skill sets needed by educators as they adjust to the ongoing expectations of their profession. Over the years, I've had to reinvent myself to match the surroundings in which I have taught. I've changed from

- A lower elementary teacher to a middle school teacher
- A core classroom teacher to a music and art specialist
- A public school teacher to a private school teacher
- A teacher of phonics to a whole-language teacher
- A math teacher who went by the book to a math teacher who used manipulatives and centers
- A technology-illiterate educator to a technology integration specialist.

Several years ago, I had the privilege of leaving my comfort zone not only in terms of pedagogy but also in terms of my cultural understanding when I taught at an Orthodox Jewish school. There, my new learning encompassed religious tradition and cultural distinctiveness. At times, I felt like a stranger in a strange land, but it was there that I came to realize I could function in a unique setting and be happy doing it.

This fall, my teaching role will be transformed once again as I become a teacher-cybrarian in a school for gifted students. Although this is once again unfamiliar territory, I look forward to seeing what new teaching form I will become in this different place. It's morphing time again!

Additional Resources

Coping With Change
http://www.itstime.com/may97a.htm

This online newsletter from The Institute of Management Excellence examines myths about change, how various personalities deal with change, and ways in which leaders can help employees deal with change.

Leading Thoughts: Quotes on Change
http://www.leadershipnow.com/changequotes.html

"Leading Thoughts" on change from Mark Twain, Peter Senge, Thomas Jefferson, and others.

The Quote Garden: Quotations About Change
http://www.quotegarden.com/change.html

Quotations that will help you view change with a positive attitude.

7.
Your Professional Development: Let Your Fingers Do the Walking

I've just spent the afternoon listening to Thomas Armstrong, a popular conference speaker and the author of *Words Come Alive: The Multiple Intelligences of Reading and Writing.*

Yesterday, I sat mesmerized by Grant Wiggins, Jay McTighe, and Carol Ann Tomlinson's *Understanding by Design and Differentiated Instruction* presentation. For a Canadian teacher who can sometimes feel a little removed from the education reform hothouse, listening to those experts share their ideas and best practices was very exciting. The best part was that my sessions with Armstrong and Wiggins didn't cost me a dime—they took place as I sat at my computer in the comfort of my home study.

Wired teachers

Those free online sessions are one example of a restructuring of professional development (PD) that is occurring within our profession. Realizing that improving student learning is dependent on teachers' continuing to learn and improve, an abundance of free or low-cost professional development opportunities are springing up on the Internet. No longer can I complain that relevant professional development is too far away, or too costly. It is as close as my fingertips. I've discovered the PD of my dreams—opportunities that meet my PD needs *and* fit into my hectic schedule, budget limitations, interests, and learning style. Gone are the days when professional development was something done *to* teachers, not *with* them!

Your personal professional development needs

For "wired" teachers, online professional development opportunities are abundant. Most teachers can find great learning options. Educators can find resources, in fact, even if they aren't sure what their professional development needs are.

The Association for Supervision and Curriculum Development (ASCD) has created a Professional Development Survey *http://www.ascd.org/ trainingopportunities/ossd/survey.cfm* to help teachers identify their strengths and pinpoint areas that might benefit from a PD improvement plan.

Read all about it online

Don't let the price of professional reading material get in the way of keeping up with the latest developments in our profession. Many magazines post large portions of their content online, and publishers are anxious to have readers browse through online versions of their books. Although most of us don't want to read complete books online, having the opportunity to read key chapters will help us decide whether the book is worth buying—and nobody said you can't learn while browsing.

The following list offers just a handful of the professional development periodicals you can browse or read online:

- *Education Week:* http://www.edweek.org/
- *Instructor:* http://teacher.scholastic.com/products/instructor/index.htm
- *Journal of Staff Development:* http://www.nsdc.org/
- *MultiMedia Schools:* http://www.infotoday.com/MMSchools/past.shtml
- *Phi Delta Kappan:* http://www.pdkintl.org/kappan/karticle.htm
- *Teacher:* http://www.teachermagazine.org/

The opportunity to browse before you buy can help educators select those books that will be most practical to purchase as desktop references. The following are among the growing list of publishers who offer excerpts or complete texts online:

- **Stenhouse Publishers:** *http://www.stenhouse.com/pdfbooks.htm*
- **Heinemann Publishers:** *http://www.heinemann.com/shared/resources/sample_chapters.asp#79*

Attend a conference—vicariously

As schools try to make shrinking funds go further, budgets for teacher travel to conferences is often trimmed, sometimes eliminated. Just in the nick of time, technology has come to the rescue. Online videos, audio files, and Webcasts enable educators to hear prominent education speakers such as Grant Wiggins, Robert Marzano, and Annette Lamb.

The following list offers a small selection of conferences that have employed technology to make conference offerings available beyond the walls of the actual conference:

- ASCD 2003 Conference (from San Francisco, California)
  http://www.simulconference.com/ASCD/2003/
- ASCD 2002 Conference (from San Antonio, Texas)
  http://www.simulconference.com/clients/ascd/

- 2003 National Educational Computing Conference (from Seattle, Washington)
  http://center.uoregon.edu/NECC/NECC2003/attendees/program/webcasting.php
- WebCasts from NMSA (from Breckenridge, Colorado; fee involved)
  http://www.nmsa.org/development/onlinecourses.htm

Go to school—at home

The Annenberg/CPB Channel is a free satellite channel that airs a range of teacher professional development and instructional programming. Their diverse courses also can be accessed online, and a number of them can be taken for graduate credit. You can view sessions such as Making Civics Real: A Workshop For Teachers, In Search of the Novel, and Mathematics: What's the Big Idea? at the link below:

- Annenberg/CPB Channel
  http://www.learner.org/channel/channel.html

Learning from one another

Building collaboration and reflection among colleagues is "on the grow" thanks to a well thought out program called Critical Friends Groups. Working together to improve their teaching practices has given the close-knit groups of educators a support system and a wealth of experience to draw on. Professional isolation is close to being extinct! You can learn more about Critical Friends Groups in an *Education World* article, "Critical Friends Groups: Catalysts for School Change" *http://www.educationworld.com/a_admin/admin136.shtml.*

Participating in a focused, vibrant listserv is one of the best professional development tools available to teachers today. The following teacher listserv resources prove that looking for guidance, ideas, and insightful conversations was never so easy.

- Teacher-2-Teacher Listserv: *http://www.teachnet.com/t2t/*
- Electronic Discussion Lists Hosted by ECAP
  Lists for many interests: *http://ecap.crc.uiuc.edu/projects.html#listserv*
- Classroom Connect's Mailing Lists: *http://listserv.classroom.com/archives/* Lists for many interests.
- MiddleWeb Listserv: *http://www.middleweb.com/mw/aaChat.html* One of the best lists for middle level teachers.
- EdTech Listserv: *http://www.h-net.org/~edweb* Discussion of educational technology issues.

8.
It's Quittin' Time

It's the end of the school year and a scene from the movie *Gone With the Wind* http://www.franklymydear.com/ keeps playing over and over in my mind. The scene takes place at the end of a hard day of work in the cotton fields. One of the field hands shouts "quittin' time" only to be rebuked by his foreman who says he'll decide "when it's quittin' time" and then immediately calls "quittin' time."

This disagreement over "quittin' time" is reminiscent of the last few weeks of school when each member of a learning community begins his or her own "quittin' time" process. Focused on the possibilities of next year, administrators and teachers cast their eyes to the fall. Influenced by their lead and the promises of summer, students begin to disengage from the learning tasks at hand.

It seems to me that "quittin' time" is starting earlier and earlier in the school year. In the interest of learning, I've been thinking about ways we might reclaim some of that lost time.

Following through is hard work

It is no small task for educators to maintain the start-of-the-school-year enthusiasm to the end of June. The demands and disappointments of the year can't help but wear us down. The challenging work that accompanies unrealized learning goals or the disillusionment that settles in when teaching initiatives flounder can slow us.

As I approach the last quarter of the school year, I notice a familiar phenomenon developing around me. Attention begins to shift towards the upcoming school year. Hiring needs, scheduling decisions, future room assignments, and think tanks about upcoming initiatives begin to absorb the attention of school administrators and teachers. Instead of continuing in our relentless pursuit of supporting students to meet success, "next year" peppers our plans and conversation. The principal's absence in the hallways is noticeable; it even becomes difficult to find a time when the door to the principal's office is open. In the classroom, wind-up programs or celebrations and filler movies start to appear in greater frequency.

I watch this end-of-year cycle unfold each year and wonder what causes the prospects of the future to be more compelling than the challenges of the present. To an onlooker, it can often appear that educators are allowing the present year to play out on its own.

Recapturing the last days of school

In a recent MiddleWeb listserv discussion, former middle school principal Michelle Pedigo expressed her belief that it is up to leadership to expect learning to continue—even on the last day the buses run. She recommended educators consider ways to use the last days of school more productively. Following are a few of the points she made:

- Do your teachers loop (move on to the next grade level with the same students)? Looping encourages teachers to continue teaching to the end of the year since they are really teaching for the next year.

- If schools audited their time, are they really doing all they can do to meet students' needs within the school calendar? Teachers complain about how much the state-mandated tests take out of instructional time, but then show movies and assign no homework during the last week of school.

- A school-wide interdisciplinary unit could be scheduled for the last two weeks of the school year. Pedigo told of a "Decades" unit her school presented one year. Each team studied a decade after World War II. They created a wide variety of presentations. Since the decade they chose was part of next year's curriculum, it allowed them to get a jumpstart on next year.

In order to make productive use of the last days of school, other MiddleWeb teachers offered the following advice:

- **Encourage students to finish well.** Allow students who need to bring up their grades time to do makeup work.

- **Make memories.** Organize a wide variety of activities—basketball and volleyball games in the gym, relay races on the field, a dunking booth, computer games, arts and crafts, chess tournaments, a movie, and anything else you might dream up. Divide the day into segments. Let students decide which activities they will participate in or have them rotate among the activities.

- **Write and reflect.** Have students write letters to the students who will be in their grade next year; in those letters they should give tidbits of insight, advice, and information.

- **Make a difference.** Involve students in community service work. Make cards for people in local nursing homes or have kids create games for younger students.

- **Keep learning.** Hold contests that involve learning, such as an egg drop competition (Egg Drop Competition *http://www.mindspring.com/~eggdrop/*) or a paper airplane flying contest.

- **Evaluate**. Ask students for feedback about some of the projects and activities done in your class over the year.

One middle school teacher expressed her motivation for teaching until quittin' time this way: "All and all, I am glad I taught until the last dog died. That is what [the students'] parents are paying me to do, and that is what I always do."

Additional Resources

Making the Most of the Dreaded End-of-School Days
http://www.educationworld.com/a_lesson/lesson268.shtml

An abundance of year-end activities from *Education World*.

Winding Up Learning as the Year Winds Down
http://www.educationworld.com/a_lesson/lesson184.shtml

Activities for the last few days of school.

Egg Drop Competition
http://www.asme.org/eggdrop/

Information about the Egg Drop contest, held as a part of Engineer's Week activities.

Quittin' Time Audio File
http://www.reelclassics.com/Movies/GWTW/GWTW.htm

Hear that memorable phrase from *Gone With the Wind!*

9.
Professional Conferences Reflect, Restore Passion

Flying at an altitude of 35,000 feet for an extended period of time seems to foster reflection—and I have plenty to reflect about as I fly back from my second teaching conference in two weeks. Last week, I participated in the National Middle School Association's (NMSA) *http://www.nmsa.org/* convention in Washington, D.C. Today, I am returning from Atlanta, where I attended the annual Technology + Learning Conference *http://www.nsba. org/T+L.*

Lest you think this globetrotting life is typical for me, I should explain that I have never before attended a teaching conference farther away than my local downtown convention center.

What, you might wonder, could possibly lure this homebody away from the comforts and safety of her classroom? I must admit that I asked myself that very same question two weeks ago when safety concerns forced me to reconsider flying to Washington. In the end, I was lured onto that plane by

- My commitment to continuous improvement
- My thirst to learn
- My desire to pick the brains of cutting-edge educators from across the continent
- My awareness that meeting with a kaleidoscope of educators would broaden my own perspective
- The opportunity to connect with many of my virtual colleagues, including members of listservs I belong to.

I was taken aback by the sheer size of the two conferences I attended. I'm used to small, local conventions. To sit in a general session with thousands of colleagues was a completely sobering experience. I was cognizant of the fact that, for many attendees, their presence at the conference represented a personal refusal to let fear interfere with their right to practice their profession; each educator stood for me as a symbol of the "spirit of America."

I expected the bulk of my learning to occur in the sessions I attended. Although those sessions *did* expose me to new ideas and excellent examples of quality learning, my most profound learning moments were encountered outside the sessions—while talking with educators across the country. From my fellow educators, I learned

- **Passion for teaching is alive and well.** If you want to get away from disenchanted educators who seek to drag you down with them, attend a teaching conference. I met dozens of educators whose passion for teaching, desire to become the best teachers they can be, and commitment to reach all kids shines bright. Sometimes that light was blinding!

- **Teachers are still the most resourceful people I know.** I gained new insights and ideas everywhere I went—even while sitting on the bus, walking to a session, or eating lunch.

- **Meeting virtual (listserv) colleagues in person is one of the greatest professional pleasures and privileges imaginable.** Over the past year, my listserv colleagues and I have supported each other through many highs and lows. The highlight of my time in Washington and in Atlanta was when I shook hands with those who have been such a source of encouragement and inspiration to me.

- **What is meant by the "digital divide."** I met teachers who carry out incredible programs in one-computer classrooms as well as teachers who are blessed with a computer or a handheld device for every student. Such inequalities troubled me.

As my plane begins its descent into my hometown airport, I wonder what I should do with the learning gleaned from my travels. I wonder what I should do with the fresh realization that exciting educational reform is taking place in everyday schools, led by unlikely teachers—teachers just like me. Could ordinary teachers like me—educators who have discovered unexpected learning breakthroughs worth sharing—even lead conference sessions?

Perhaps education conferences are not just places for talking. Maybe they also provide an opportunity for us to give back something to our profession.

Additional Resource

Debate Rages Over Digital Divide
http://www.educationworld.com/a_admin/admin103.shtml

Are your students "haves" or "have-nots"? Are they tech savvy or are they being left behind because your school hasn't kept pace with technology? Explore the "digital divide" in this special *Education World* story.

10.
Where Have All the Staff Rooms Gone?

On days when I'm gulping my sandwich and balancing my juice box as I supervise lunch hour hallways, my mind floats back to the lunch hours I experienced as a beginning teacher in the 1970s. Back then, staff rooms were happening places. There were never enough chairs, and the coffee urn was big enough to float a navy.

The staff room action began each morning as teachers congregated to visit before the school day began. The smell of toast and coffee wafted through the air. During recess, teachers scurried down for a quick chat and a coffee.

The best part of staff room life happened at lunchtime, however. Because lunchroom supervisors tended to students, teachers could take advantage of an uninterrupted break. Even telephone calls didn't intrude into the first half of the lunch hour; the school secretary took messages. I was part of a teacher's choir that met once a week during that time—just for the joy of singing together. Some teachers changed into shorts and went for a jog or played volleyball. On Fridays, we jumped into cars and headed for a favorite local restaurant. All of us looked forward to that time to share a meal and talk about the week's teaching experiences. To this day, I can't eat a club sandwich without thinking of those teaching colleagues.

Are staff rooms extinct?

Today, I teach down the hall from an abandoned staff room. The lights are off, the chairs are empty, and only a small coffeepot sits brewing on the counter. The room is so seldom used that there is talk of converting it into an extra classroom. Whatever happened?

More than ever, teachers are on the go from the moment they arrive at school until long past the last bell. Camaraderie in the staff room has been replaced by a new trend—the working lunch, a break more about working than lunching. Multitasking has become our new mantra. Instead of chatting uninterrupted, we balance bowls of soup on our laps as we answer e-mails. We munch a sandwich while supervising volleyball in the gym. When we finally get a moment to ourselves, we hole up in our classroom to prep for the next class of students.

Rediscovering the staff room

Last week, two very disabling viruses hit my school's computer network. For most of the week, we couldn't access our files, e-mail, or the Internet. We couldn't even print. One lunch hour, I threw up my hands in frustration and wandered down to our staff room.

As I approached the long-abandoned area, I heard some unfamiliar sounds. They sounded vaguely like...laughter. I turned to open the door and was treated to a scene reminiscent of the 1970s—a room full of teaching colleagues. They were eating together and enjoying one another's company.

You would have thought they had just discovered something very new. I, for one, hope we have.

> *Great individuals don't make great teams unless they build good working relationships. Having the right ingredients —the right mix of people, skills, resources—is essential but not enough. Without the right relationships, even "All Stars" can't win.*
>
> —Wayne E. Baker

Additional Resources

Bowling Alone: The Collapse and Revival of American Community
http://www.bowlingalone.com/index.php3

Author Robert Putnam reveals the power of social capital —the belief that social networks have value—and proposes that America has lost much of the "social glue" that allowed us to prosper in the past.

What Does Social Capital Mean?
http://www.bowlingalone.com/socialcapital.php3

Social capital emphasizes not just warm and cuddly feelings, but a wide variety of benefits that flow from trust, reciprocity, and information.

Better Together
http://www.bettertogether.org/index.htm

Congregating in a staff room will take on a whole new meaning after exploring this Web site from the Saguaro Seminar.

150 Things You Can Do to Create Social Capital.
http://www.bettertogether.org/150ways.htm

The main principle of social capital is that social networks have value. Try some of these on your own or with your staff.

Celebration and Events to Build the Team
http://www.teambuildinginc.com/article_celebrations.htm

11.
About Stephen...and Fresh Starts

Each season is a new beginning, a new way of thinking. Hope is perched on every branch; dreams are whispered in the wind, nature hears our call."

--- Jane Dalton, teacher

My childhood memories of beginning a new school year are full of new clothes, new binders and pencils, and, best of all, a new class and teacher. Each year held the promise of a fresh beginning. Gone were the failures of the previous year.

How well I remember the resolutions I made each summer, those private oaths to do better than I had in the past. "This year," I would tell myself, "I will keep up with my work, watch less TV, start my homework earlier, and try to focus better during class."

The year I entered grade 11 was a year of promises made like every other. I knew that unless I made some significant changes in my work habits and my attitude, my chances of passing my math class were slim. I passed, barely, but I know that those beginning of the year resolutions—and my ability to act on them—were what got me through math that year. I might have had only a 65 at the end of the course, but my ability to change my work habits and attitudes taught me an unforgettable lesson: I possessed the power within myself to make necessary changes in my life.

A new day

This week, I've been thinking about all those students who will be returning to school this fall. Just like I used to do, many are thinking about what went wrong in their past school experiences. Some are even contemplating academic and behavioral changes they might make. More sobering, some are wondering if change is even possible, especially if the teachers they will have this year have been given a "heads up" about their past follies.

Do teachers give each student a chance to begin fresh each year? I'm not so sure. After sitting through my share of report-outs about incoming students, I wonder why teachers are so determined to share the negative information they know about their students. While it is helpful for me to know about my students' academic and health challenges, I would prefer to have the freedom to begin my year with little knowledge about their past mistakes. Some might think this lack of information could put me at a disadvantage, but I would like to look at my students with fresh eyes. I hope to give every one of them the opportunity to make a fresh start.

The power of fresh starts

Thirty years ago this month, I began my first year of teaching. One of the most memorable aspects of that first year was a little boy in my grade two classroom who exhibited severe ADHD characteristics. I had no training in dealing with special needs cases like Stephen, and I spent the year learning by trial and error how to help this eight-year-old become a successful learner. There were many frustrating moments, but there was something very endearing about that little boy who buzzed haphazardly around my classroom.

As the end of the school year approached, I heard the talk. The grade three teachers were shuddering at the thought of having Stephen next year. The more I thought about it, the more I realized that I would be the best person to loop with Stephen into grade three. My principal looked at me with disbelief when I made my request to follow Stephen into the next grade, but he agreed to my plan.

I will never forget that day in September when Stephen came to ask why he was in my class again. I looked him square in the eye and I said, *"Well Stephen, you're in my class because I asked for you."* The little guy peeking out from under a pile of tousled black hair looked stunned. *"You did? Why?"* he asked. *"Because I like you and want to keep working with you,"* I responded.

Stephen just stared at me. After a few moments, he smiled and wandered back to his seat. We never spoke of it again, but the two of us had many incredible learning breakthroughs that year. I believe those successes were more a result of Stephen knowing that I had put his previous year's mistakes behind him than in any special teaching technique I used.

Or maybe it had more to do with what poet, Langston Hughes so astutely observed: *"When people care for you and cry for you, they can straighten out your soul."*

Grabbing the moment

Teachers begin each school year with a brief window of opportunity. Many students coming into our classes desire a fresh start and are primed to act upon it. Knowing that, we need to be watchful for even the smallest indication that students are looking for help to carry out improvement oaths made during the summer. Our role needs to be one of a cheerleader and a task manager, never a naysayer.

IV. Technology

It's not just about the technology, it's also about changing how we approach and design learning in the classroom.

— Justine K. Brown

1.
Stand By Me: Using Teacher Listservs to Collaborate With Other Educators

One of my favorite historical images is that of Franklin D. Roosevelt and Winston Churchill standing at the South Portico of the White House on Christmas Eve 1941. They have just sent mutual Christmas greetings to the people of the United States.

Brought together by World War II, the two world leaders created an unexpected collaborative relationship, one that would eventually prompt Roosevelt to cable Churchill, "It is fun to be in the same decade with you."

Now, 60 years later, as I reflect on my own collaborative experiences with teacher listservs, I have to say that I share Roosevelt's sentiments. Bonded by the goal of effectively reaching and teaching today's young people, my virtual colleagues and I have developed enjoyable, productive, and professional relationships that stretch from Canada to Australia, from the United States to the Middle East, and to and from all places in between. Using the Internet, we communicate regularly, support one another unconditionally, celebrate one another's successes, and mentor one another constantly—in spite of the apparent obstacle of global separation.

Learning to collaborate

It didn't start out that way, of course. My initial listserv activities resembled the old-fashioned pen pal scenarios that most of us experienced in our youth. After registering on a listserv, I casually shared ideas, lesson plans, and stories from my classroom.

Before long, however, I began to realize that the people I was communicating with weren't your typical pen pals. They were serious educators looking for ways to improve their teaching practices. They were intelligent, reflective, and their pedagogy was up to date.

My first true exposure to "global mentoring"—one teacher helping another teacher via the Internet—happened the day I offered to share a unit I had created on the theme of heroes. In one day, I received requests for that unit from more than 100 teachers! The requests came from places as far away as Australia and as close as a town 200 miles from my home. Because I didn't realize I could just post the Web page address on the listserv, I spent the next day e-mailing each and every teacher.

I was amazed at the level of trust and commitment that many listserv members were willing to demonstrate to colleagues who were perfect strangers. A teacher from California sent me $138 so I could buy her the same flashy technology fabric—covered with illustrations of various technology tools—I had used as a background on classroom bulletin boards. Another teacher sent me a video of a program she had written about in one of her listserv postings. One teacher even offered to spend the weekend re-formatting my Web pages so pop-up ads didn't continue to distract the reader.

It quickly became evident to me that I no longer needed to handle all my classroom challenges on my own. Answers to my daily classroom dilemmas were as close as my listserv community. A powerful level of professional camaraderie developed among my listserv colleagues. Soon I had more meaningful professional relationships with virtual colleagues than I had with many of my peers in my own school.

Taking collaboration to a new level
The day I got off the plane in Raleigh, North Carolina, I knew I had crossed over from virtual collaboration to collaboration in the "here and now." As a result of my online work with students and educators, I had been selected to be a teacher-editor with *MidLink Magazine*, an e-zine that profiles innovative online classroom projects *http://www.cs.ucf. edu/~MidLink/*. I traveled to Raleigh to meet and work with MidLink's team of teacher-editors *http://www.ncsu.edu/midlink/ml.eds/ml.eds.2000.bio.htm* to take a collaborative relationship begun online to a deeper level. I left Raleigh inspired and better equipped to integrate technology into my classroom projects.

Since that first trip to North Carolina, I have had the opportunity to meet many more of my listserv colleagues at international learning conferences. I am always amazed at how easy it is to connect and how quickly we move from small talk to the topics that drew us together in the first place—education reform and technology integration.

Like Roosevelt and Churchill, my listserv friends and I have discovered that by merging minds, cultural differences, and resources, we are able to achieve a common good that might, at the end of the day, be education's "finest hour."

Additional Resources

Looking for a listserv?

Following are a handful of resources to help educators learn more about listservs.

- Teacher-to-Teacher Listserv
  http://www.teachnet.com/t2t/
  This multi-grade listserv is a terrific place to start listserv life.

- MiddleWeb Listserv
  http://www.middleweb.com/MWlistserve.html
  Discover one of the most active, thought-provoking listservs for middle level educators on the Net.

- For a World of Help, Try a Listserv
  http://www.masters.ab.ca/bdyck/listserv/
  Another article by Brenda Dyck offers further information on teacher listservs.

- Getting Started on the Internet: Add Your Name to a Listserv —Today
  http://www.educationworld.com/a_curr/curr062.shtml
  In this 1998 *Education World* article, learn what a listserv is and how it can benefit you.

More about Roosevelt and Churchill

http://www.archives.gov/digital_classroom/lessons/fdr_churchill_documents/fdr_churchill.html

This lesson about the close friendship and working relationship that developed between U.S. President Franklin D. Roosevelt and British Prime Minister Winston Churchill includes the text of their Christmas Eve greetings.

2.
Learning in the Dark:
Building My First Web Project and Web Page

I closed my classroom door and walked down the vacated halls of my school. Everyone had gone home for the summer holidays, and I had just put the finishing touches on my first-ever telecollaborative project Web page. Never in my wildest dreams did I think I would be able to design and manage my own project, let alone create a Web page to house the resulting student work.

My telecollaborative project began with a small idea—a social studies assignment that I thought might beef up my humdrum government unit. My sixth graders would brainstorm qualities that strong leaders might possess; then they would reflect on those qualities as they used Internet resources to learn more about former and current government leaders.

With hesitancy, I submitted my project idea to SchoolNet GrassRoots, a government organization that offers funding to Canadian teachers who create collaborative and interactive learning projects on the Internet. To my surprise, my project idea, "I'm Leading, Is Anyone Following?" was accepted.

Get the word out!

I needed to figure out a way to get teachers and their students to actually join the project and quickly realized that the Net was the ideal tool for locating teachers who might partner with my class. I put out a call for participation on as many education sites and listservs as I could. To my delight, six Canadian and three American classrooms joined in. I also heard from Caroline McCullen, editor of *MidLink Magazine*, an online education magazine. *MidLink* profiles online learning projects that reflect the creative learning process in technology-rich classrooms. Caroline invited me to post my project on *MidLink Magazine's* Web site *http://www.cs.ucf.edu/~MidLink/*.

I knew that the success of this project hinged on how well I could articulate the thinking behind "I'm Leading, Is Anyone Following?" To that end, I used the Yahoo eGroup feature to create an eGroup where the teachers I had recruited could share thoughts, resources, and suggestions for implementation. We used that tool to get to know one another and to iron out project glitches.

Posting the students' work

Finally, it was time to build the Web pages. I was determined to bravely tread where I'd never been before. I was going to use *FrontPage 2000* to create the Web pages; so I bought Ruth Maran's book, *FrontPage 2000 Simplified*, and followed the pictures step by step. I asked tons of questions and made just as many mistakes.

Soon the project teachers started sending student work to me, and I began to build the Web pages. As my confidence increased, so did my Web page plans. Plain Web pages were replaced with e-mail links, sound, tables, and thumbnail images. I actually started to understand what I was doing!

By far, the most satisfying part of my first telecollaborative adventure was reading the student writing as it came in from Florida, Saskatchewan, British Columbia, and Alberta. It was amazing to me that distance had not gotten in the way of the learning. In fact, the project seemed to be enhanced by the distance and cultural diversity that each classroom brought to its submissions. The students' voices were there, along with evidence of higher-level thinking. The project had turned out just as I had envisioned it a year before. The "I'm Leading, Is Anyone Following?" Web page stood as a testament to student learning—and to my own learning as well.

Additional Resources

Brenda's and Robin's Tech Tips
http://www.microsoft.com/education/?ID=TeacherTechTipsArchive

This site offers this "ultimate technology handholding guide," which the authors describe as "a year's worth of advice for making technology part of your teaching."

FrontPage 2000 Simplified
http://www.amazon.com/exec/obidos/ASIN/0764534505/qid%3D1000523797/103-2839376-8336613

This book, by Ruth Maran, presents step-by-step, full color instructions for using Microsoft's popular Web design package. A great resource for beginners.

Yahoo eGroups
http://groups.yahoo.com/local/news.html

Learn to implement eGroups in your communication with colleagues and students at this resource from Yahoo.

3.
Seeing is Believing:
Harnessing Online Video Clips to Enhance Learning

Squeezing a high-tech learning environment into a 1940s classroom can be like forcing a round peg into a square hole. Electrical outlets are at a premium; blowing a fuse can be a daily event! But, whenever I am down on my knees searching for an electrical outlet, my mind floats back to the classrooms of my past. I can still remember how much I looked forward to filmstrip presentations—and the even bigger rarity, a 35mm film.

I still recall the day a film about pygmies arrived at our school. The whole school watched, mesmerized, even though nobody was studying about pygmies. And I will never forget that November day in 1963 when three classes crammed into our small classroom so that we all could watch President Kennedy's funeral on our school TV. Over the next few years, more films were brought into our classrooms. With the advent of the VCR, educational television followed.

How could someone like me from the filmstrip generation, ever have envisioned a day when I would search for unused outlets and for ways to connect to curriculum content with Net-Generation students who have been surrounded by digital media since they took their first breaths?

Connecting with a different generation

Most teachers have come to understand that Net-Geners relate best to curriculum when teachers incorporate the medium that captivates them the most—video—to help translate abstract concepts or events into their reality.

Once again, the Internet has come to my rescue. On the Net I have discovered access to a library of video clips relevant to my curriculum—video that inspires, challenges, and teaches. Using a projector connected to a computer, the content of those clips can be experienced by my students and myself. Those clips open up tremendous opportunities for meaningful dialogue.

The Web can transport learners to places and times long ago. It offers experiences that bring history to life in ways no other medium can. Via the Internet, my students can

- Wander through the catacombs behind the Western Wall in Jerusalem *http://www.aish.com/seminars/tunneltour/ and get an interactive view of the wall http://www.inisrael.com/3disrael/kotel/*

- Meander along the Great Wall of China *http:// www.thebeijingguide.com/great_wall_of_china/index.html*
- Tour Ellis Island *http://www.historychannel.com/ellisisland/* as they listen to testimonials by people who arrived there.

Many of the sites my students visit via the Internet challenge their mental models, blast cultural stereotypes, and inspire them to explore in depth the people, places, and events of history.

Unleash student voices

Short, powerful messages can stir even the most complacent student to act. The Web offers a huge library of video created for that purpose. In the classroom, that video can prompt discussion, inspire writing, and create emotional connections that will stick with students for a long time. The following online video offerings provide just a few examples:

- World Against Child Labor *http://www.ilo.org/public/english/bureau/ inf/childlabour/index.htm*
- The Power of One is a short video clip *http:// www.caringstrangers.com/powerofone.htm* that features historical and contemporary persons whose efforts illustrate how every one of us can make a difference.

History comes alive

Net-Geners are used to seeing historical events unfold before their eyes. The Web offers an abundance of historical film and audio from which students can learn about and experience events long before their time. The following are a few excellent sources of historical video:

- National Holocaust Museum: *http://www.ushmm.org*

  The National Holocaust Museum Film and Video Archive includes 420 hours of motion picture footage (primarily from the 1920s to 1948). Here students can view video of large crowds gathered for Adolf Hitler's arrival at the Nazi party rally in Nuremberg, Germany (September 1937) as well as attacks against Jewish property and family life.

- American Field Guide: A library of more than 1,400 video clips *http://www.pbs.org/americanfieldguide* enables students to experience America's wilderness.

- The Veteran Experience: *http://www.historychannel.com/cgi-bin/ frameit.cgi?p=http://www.historychannel.com/exhibits/memorial/vetex.html*

  View video of American veterans as they share their war memories.

- The History Channel's Speech Archive *http://
  www.historychannel.com/speeches/index.html*

  Hear the words that changed the world.

Up-to-date Internet access allows teachers to seize countless learning opportunities. Through video news clips, students are able to get instant answers to their questions about history or the most current of current events. The following sites provide excellent sources of video relating to today's top news stories:

- Frontline *http://www.pbs.org/wgbh/pages/frontline*

  This documentary series from PBS exposes readers to investigative journalism. The topics are often controversial, and the videos challenge students' critical thinking skills. Useful teacher guides are included.

- CNN *http://www.cnn.com*

  Find video relating to up-to-the-moment breaking news stories.

4.
In Classrooms, Computers Often Yield More Glitz Than Guts

We live in a world where there is more and more information, and less and less meaning.

—Jean Baudrillard

For some, teaching in a school where all teachers have laptops and where classrooms are loaded with networked computers may seem like a dream come true. After spending time in such a technology-rich environment, however, I realize that there's more to this dream than the fun and freedom that accompanies technology.

It is so easy to under-utilize technology tools which, when used to their fullest potential, could enable students to visit places they might never see, support critical thinking in a multitude of ways, and provide opportunities to experience intercultural collaboration. The effectiveness of technology is watered down when the laptops are used solely for basic word processing, haphazard surfing, or creating jazzed-up PowerPoint presentations.

When I look back at my beginning attempts at technology integration, I can see that I settled for student projects comprised of a whole lot of glitz and not a lot of guts. At first I was impressed with the technology-injected results—but that was before I looked more closely at the lack of depth in the student-created content, the overload of bells and whistles in their presentations, and in some cases, the blatant plagiarism.

Mind candy

Jamie McKenzie, editor of *From Now On: The Educational Technology Journal* http://www.fno.org/, warns teachers about the emergence of what he calls "mind candy" http://www.fno.org/jun98/kafe.html

> We see eye candy making its way into schools as multimedia presentations, "full of sound and fury, often signifying nothing." I remember watching two fifth graders presenting a PowerPoint report on tigers that employed every known transition and special effect the software offered. Content? It was very slim, indeed. Even less information than we have come to expect from one

of those time-honored encyclopedia-based reports. There was little thinking or information value here. But the special effects were impressive. ... When it came time for a picture of a tiger, unable to find one, they substituted a picture of a lion! No explanation. No excuses. No footnote. And no one seemed to notice or care. After all—they were both members of the cat family!

Getting to the "mind meat"

I began to see some improvement in the quality of technology integration in my program once students' project work required them to create their own information by using data from the Web or using e-mail to communicate with peers in other places. Improvements continued once I started creating assignments that included broad questions designed to lead students toward new knowledge and understandings.

"Fluttering Butterflies," a project created by a first-year teacher at my school, is an excellent example of a project that shifted students beyond the mere summarization of facts. In this science project, students used a word processing program to keep logs in which they documented their observations about classroom butterflies. Not only did this project provide a platform for young students to hone their observation skills, it also fostered the process of "meaning making" in these beginning learners.

This year I also had the opportunity to work with a teacher whose objective was to push the boundaries of static course delivery. In his G8 Summit Simulation, students used the Internet to collect basic background information about the June 2002 summit of world leaders. Students applied that knowledge as they took on hypothetical roles in a simulation that addressed such real-life concerns as the environment, military disarmament, global economics, international terrorism, and political unrest. This assignment had the makings of an exciting collaborative project, one that could open up debate opportunities among students in other countries. Students could further apply their technology skills by staging a debate on an Internet messaging service such as Windows Messenger *http://messenger.msn.com* or on a virtual bulletin board such as Yahoo! Groups *http://groups.yahoo.com.*

It's all about how we *use* the tools

I'm reminded of a phrase used by our colleague Dr. Judi Harris. She says, "It's not about how we use the *tools*. It's (mostly) about how we *use* the tools."

As a technology enthusiast, I am easily diverted by the prospects of having a class set of computers, the most up-to-date techno gizmos, cyber this, and cyber that. If my overall goal is to use technology to help students think in newer, deeper ways, I must periodically step back to re-evaluate my purpose and the depth of learning I see in the students who spend time in my wired classroom.

Additional Resources

Laptop Computers for Every Student
http://www.educationworld.com/a_curr/curr048.shtml

Read what it is like to have a class set of computers.

Scoring Power Points
http://www.fno.org/sept00/powerpoints.html

This article by Jamie McKenzie shows how to keep the "power" in *PowerPoint*.

5.
Telecollaborative Project
Develops Compassion, Global Awareness

*There is a great difference between knowing and
understanding: You can know a lot about something and
not really understand it.* —Charles F. Kettering

M iddle school students seem to be walking contradictions. They're
gregarious one moment and guarded the next. They exhibit
incredible curiosity while their body language oozes boredom. They
treasure individuality even though they frequently choose to move
in mirror-image herds. To tap into the authentic side of middle school
students, you almost need to catch them off guard. I've discovered that
it is during a moment of surprise that middle school students often
demonstrate vulnerability, wisdom, deep authenticity, and compassion.
Recently, I caught two classes, from opposite sides of the globe, off guard.

For several months, my class has been working with a group of
students from Israel on a telecollaborative project called We the Children...
For this project, both classes explored one of the most basic human rights
—the right to a safe place. For part of the project, students immersed
themselves in identifying the characteristics of a safe classroom. They used
those criteria to evaluate their classroom and their country in general.

During this time, the Canadian and Israeli students e-mailed back and
forth. The conversations focused on the issues and activities that concern
most 13- and 14-year-olds—sports, music, weekend activities, and fashion.
Throughout the e-mail correspondence, my students and I were perplexed
that no one spoke of or even alluded to the frequent terrorist attacks in
Israel.

It wasn't until both classes of students handed in their reflective
writing that a sobering picture of two very different living environments
began to emerge. Using poetry as the format, the Israeli students began
to describe the unsafe setting they call home. They told of being afraid of
going into the street, attending movies protected by guards, and not being
free to use buses or take trips.

One student, Sharon, described the reality of her unsafe world and then fantasized about living in Chicago, a place she considered very safe. Gilat reflected on living in Switzerland, a place she considered to be at peace with the entire world. The poignancy of her words will always stick in my mind:

> My teacher asked a question once:
> Which country do you think is the safest one?
> Dan said France, Nurit said England,
> Yuval said Spain, I said Switzerland.
> I am not sure, but I was told
> That Switzerland is at peace with all the world.
> Can you imagine this lovely thing?

I began to realize that beneath the light-hearted exterior of these students' e-mails was a generation of fearful young adults trying to make sense of the everyday terrorism around them. Like my own students, they had become very good at masking the hurtful things in their lives by covering them up with humor, sullenness, and pranks.

I caught my own students off guard the day they sat at the computers watching a CNN photo essay depicting the recent terrorism in Israel. Up to this point, they had viewed their Israeli peers as they would any other 13- or 14-year-olds. I attributed this to receiving e-mails from Israel void of any mention of the suicide bombings or the violence that is part of daily life in Israel. As students flipped through the CNN images of chaos and bombings in Tel Aviv and Jerusalem, you could have heard a pin drop.

During the debriefing session with students, our dialogue was solemn. One boy told of a peace rally he had attended at his synagogue that week and read parts of the program to the class. Another student commented that our telecollaborative project had helped her appreciate the safety of her country. She observed that studying alongside students in another culture had allowed her to make a personal connection with the people behind the unrest in Israel. This new revelation made it impossible for her to listen to news reports of suicide bombings in Israel with the same sense of detachment she had experienced before. Now she wondered whether her friend has been caught in the midst of the terrorism and was hurt.

As I looked at their serious faces and read their passionate words, I realized that telecollaborative learning not only had broadened my students' worldview but also had caused in-depth learning and compassion to penetrate their hearts.

Additional Resources

We the Children Project Page
http://www.masters.ab.ca/bdyck/Rights/index.html

Student Writing from Israel
http://www.masters.ab.ca/bdyck/Rights/Israel/index.html

Activity Structures
http://www.2learn.ca/Projects/Together/structures.html

Activity Structures are ways in which educators can envision, then organize and develop effective, meaningful telecollaborative projects for their students. This resource was designed by Dr. Judi Harris, a respected leader in technology integration.

Epals
http://www.epals.com/

Use Epals to expand your students' global awareness.

6.
Becoming a Wired Teacher

When I tell people that I am becoming a wired teacher, I get some odd responses. Thinking that it means I'm "stressed out," my listener will usually share his or her own stressors along with suggestions for stress management. Others, who think I'm speaking of the high energy I bring to my teaching, proceed to applaud my efforts and ask how I do it.

The truth is, becoming a wired teacher stems from a deep philosophical belief that technology has the potential to enhance not only my students' learning, but my own professional development as well.

This all-encompassing belief in the positive impact that technology can have began with me as a quiet hunch. The hunch grew and intensified as I started to observe the results of injecting Internet-related activities into my project assignments, writing my own curriculum-specific online projects, and eventually collaborating globally with other classrooms.

Becoming a wired teacher is more of a process than a destination. My beginning steps were small and cautious ones; my later strides were more adventurous and confident. My latest adventure has led me from scouting out new learning for myself to sharing my learning with others.

Creating a wired teachers' group

The idea to share my learning with my colleagues actually started with my principal. Although she didn't completely understand what technology integration was, she did know that what I was doing in the classroom was grabbing student interest and producing some interesting results. She believed the wonder of technology integration could be communicated with our staff if I could just spend some extended time with teachers who had so much as a beginning interest. One of the key components of this plan was her belief that unless the school was willing to provide release time from the classroom, teachers would just view technology integration as another responsibility to add to an already overwhelming job description.

Determined to get started, she fired off an e-mail to the staff asking for volunteers to consider becoming part of a wired teachers' group, an initiative that would be supported with release time from their classroom teaching. Eight teachers accepted the challenge, and I began the task of thinking through how I would mentor this group

Getting wired

Working with a group of teachers who are keen to learn all you have to share is an incredibly rewarding experience. Most of these prospective wired teachers began with an adequate level of technology skill, so their progress has been fast and profound. Their goal was to take a unit of study from their curriculum and translate it into an online project that would challenge their students' thinking.

As we proceeded, a real sense of camaraderie developed among the participants as they learned and refined their integration skills. The day their first Web page went live was a time of collaborative congratulations for all of us.

Over the past few months, teachers have implemented their projects with their students and posted the resulting work online. At the end of the year, we will share our learning with our colleagues at an after-school reception. What a wonderful time of celebration that will be!

It's been fun to watch the curiosity that our wired teachers group has created within our school. Teachers frequently wander into our sessions to listen and watch. Some even ask when the next wired teachers group will run. I have a sneaking suspicion that the next time our principal sends an e-mail asking for volunteers, we may have an onslaught of responses.

Additional Resources

Global Schoolhouse Shared Learning Teacher Awards
http://www.gsnaward.org/

Here is a list of exemplary wired teachers from the Global Net Foundation.

Integrating Technology into Instruction
http://www.infotoday.com/MMSchools/mar00/robertson.htm

This article addresses the questions "How am I going to teach this unit using technology?" or "How can I use the Internet to keep my students interested and showing up for class?"

Visions of Online Projects Dance in My Head
http://www.infotoday.com/MMSchools/jan98/story.htm

Veteran teacher, Leni Donlan, tells how technology magic has entered her professional life in the past decade.

Compiling a Profile of Staff Technology Skills
http://www.infotoday.com/MMSchools/jan02/anderson.htm

7.
Luring Learners—Against the Odds

"Do you think you can maintain discipline?" asked the superintendent." Of course I can," replied Stuart. "I'll make the work interesting and the discipline will take care of itself." —From E.B. White's *Stuart Little*

If I didn't know better, I would think that E.B. White eavesdropped on a meeting I had last fall with my principal concerning the new teaching assignment I would undertake after the New Year. Like Stuart Little, I had been asked to take over a challenging class of seventh graders—kids who were pushing the boundaries and floundering in their ability to focus. My response to this challenge was much like Stuart's: "I'll make the work interesting, and the discipline will take care of itself!"

As I planned, however, I wondered if my response had been a little too optimistic. Was it actually possible to re-engage a class that had gotten off track? I decided to approach this situation by creating an online collaborative project that would lure those learners back into the fold.

Identifying the lure

Curriculum-specific online projects can help a teacher determine the unique learning needs of a particular group of students. I ascertained that a general lack of respect and recognition of individuals had contributed to the decline of this learning environment. Keeping in mind that today's learners connect best to authentic tasks, I searched the Net for real-life happenings that might create a jumping off point for a study on respect and rights. I knew I had struck gold when I read that in May 2002 the United Nations had scheduled a special meeting to examine the success of the 1989 Convention on the Rights of the Child. I learned that young people from around the world represented their peers in New York City in an effort to provide feedback concerning whether the rights of children was a reality or just rhetoric.

Linking luring to learning

This was the beginning of "We the Children..."—a project in which students would prepare (hypothetically) to be one of the young people present at the United Nations conference in May 2002. Their job would be to develop a speech voicing their findings about children's rights in their immediate environment and the world at large. The project content set the stage for students to learn about one of the most basic rights, the "Right to a Safe Place." Students would evaluate the safety level of their classroom environment and consider such complicated issues as "What happens when your rights interfere with the rights of others?" The project links directed students to sites that provided them with background on the 41 core articles of the Convention on the Rights of the Child as well as a virtual art gallery where young people from around the world expressed themselves about children's issues and rights through various artistic media. My students wrote about "Safe Places," produced poetry about their place in our classroom, communicated their feelings via a creative medium, and created a speech to deliver to the UN. Their poetry was published online, and they learned how to create a Web page to house their final assignment.

Lessons learned while luring

Technology-rich activities clearly piqued student interest. Within a short time, most behavior issues faded and made way for the quality student work that I knew this group was capable of. The powerful Internet links created knowledge background that enabled students to apply critical thinking skills and create insightful writing. Having their work published online created a sense of pride for both students and parents. Could it be that Stuart Little was referring to technology integration when he said, "I'll make the work interesting and the discipline will take care of itself"?

Additional Resources

United Nations Convention on the Rights of the Child
http://www.savethechildren.org.uk/rightonline/whats.html

Background information and links.

United Nations Special Session on Children
http://www.unicef.org/specialsession/

Information about the May 2002 session, plus links and data.

2LearnProjectCenter
http://www.2learn.ca/Projects/ProjectCentre/projframe.html

The Project Center is a part of the larger 2Learn.ca site. The project section provides information on different aspects of telecollaborative projects plus a database of registered projects.

8.
Teacher, Alias Telementor

telementor -- conduct a mentoring relationship via a
medium of telecommunications (such as e-mail)

A s a teacher, you get used to knocks at the door.

Can we work in your room?
Can I use the phone?
Is one of your computers free?
Have you seen my binder?

Last month, I heard a different knock. This one didn't come from the hall, however. It came from Argentina via the Internet.

Hello! My name is Gonzalo. I am 16 and live in Mendoza,
Argentina. I read about your "Beyond Wild Justice" project. I
would like to join your group. Please tell me what I have to do
to start. Thanks for trusting me!

Opportunity is often difficult to recognize, and it frequently takes the form of an interruption or additional work. Because of that, I almost turned down Gonzalo's request. After all, he didn't have a teacher working with him. Who would answer his questions? Who would guide him through the project? Who would grade his work?

Captivated by Gonzalo's sincere desire to learn, however, I agreed to lead him through my telecollaborative project "Beyond Wild Justice."

New territory

During the next few weeks, a barrage of questions played in my mind. How do you set the stage for a writing assignment when the student is on the other side of the world? How do you establish a relationship when written words are the only vehicle of communication?

Once again, the same tool that introduced me to Gonzalo came to my aid. Frequent e-mails, Internet resources, scanners, and Web page publishing tools filled in the communication gap created by physical distance.

Through our e-mail correspondence I learned about a part of the world I had no knowledge of. I learned that Gonzalo lived at the foot of the Andes Mountains in Argentina. He explained that extreme weather conditions prevail there—very cold winters, very hot summers, intense dry spells, and lengthy rainstorms. In his characteristic descriptive style, Gonzalo told me that Mendoza *http://www.mendoza.com/*, the province where he lives, is a "desert turned into an oasis by God's hands." As we exchanged Internet-based information about our respective cities, I found myself starting to get a clearer understanding of the background this boy was bringing to my "class."

The learning connection

In joining the "Beyond Wild Justice" project, Gonzalo became part of a larger group of learners examining the groundbreaking legal case in which middle school bullies were charged in a case of a 14-year-old student who committed suicide. The activities and resources exposed him to the concept of restorative justice, a form of justice that seeks healing for both the victim and the perpetrator.

Throughout our e-mails I posed to Gonzalo the same soul-searching questions I would have offered my own students. The responses from Argentina often caught me off guard. Gonzalo wrote:

In your last e-mail, you told me to think about people who have returned good for evil. Since I read your email this morning, I cannot stop thinking about how hard it is for someone who has received evil to turn it into good. Then I realized [that] most important of all is to think further than the question. Do I know anyone who has returned good for evil? For me, the real question would be, am I able to return good for evil? I'm still thinking about the answer.

The power of motivation

My questions about whether a student could maintain his learning zeal without the daily monitoring of a teacher came to a standstill when Gonzalo started submitting his work. Realizing that I wouldn't be there to watch him do the Power of Words assignment *http://www.masters.ab.ca/ bdyck/Justice/Web page/QUOTES/index.html*, Gonzalo created a response-style Web page *http://www.masters.ab.ca/bdyck/Justice/Survey/survey.htm* to communicate his thoughts. His idea was amazing—one I had never even considered.

Later, Gonzalo submitted a Quilt of Forgiveness square *http:// www.masters.ab.ca/bdyck/Justice/Quilt2/Argentina/index.html* that demonstrated his ability to turn ideas of peace, forgiveness, and restoration into abstract symbols.

As I posted Gonzalo's last writing assignment—As I See It—on a Web page *http://www.masters.ab.ca/bdyck/Justice/Studentwork/Argentina/index.html*, I was astounded by this boy's depth of thought and how he had connected to the thinking behind the restorative justice movement. I could tell he really understood that when we make the effort to extend restitution to a perpetrator, the result may be a change of heart in that person—something so much more powerful than punitive justice. In Gonzalo's words,

As I was working on the different project assignments, I was feeling like I really had been there when all this happened. In the beginning, I felt like an intruder, but now I feel I was there because I did work on this project with all my soul, head, and heart.

It was now clear to me that my role as telementor had much more to do with being a navigator and encourager than being part of the watch guard.

Additional Resources

International Telementor Organization
http://www.telementor.org

A program that maximizes youth potential through academic mentoring.

National Mentoring Month 2003
http://www.whitehouse.gov/news/releases/2003/01/20030102-4.html

http://www.whitehouse.gov/news/releases/2004/01/20040109-12.html

Read about President George W. Bush's decision to name January National Mentoring Month.

National Mentoring Partnership
http://www.mentoring.org/index.adp

A site devoted to connecting youth with positive role models.

9.
Connecting Students to Their Past:
World War I Project

Time is running out. Last month, Charles Reaper, one of the last surviving infantry veterans of the Battle of Vimy Ridge *http://collections. ic.gc.ca/turner/ar_vimy.html*, died at the age of 103. With so few veterans of World War I still alive, who will share their stories? Who will help the next generation remember?

As I search for an answer to that question, I am reminded of a poignant scene from the movie *Dead Poet's Society*. Teacher John Keating has brought his class to a museum-like picture gallery containing the dusty images of students long since departed from the school. In a husky voice he whispers:

> *They're not that different from you, are they? Same haircuts. Full of hormones, just like you. Invincible, just like you feel. The world is their oyster. They believe they're destined for great things, just like many of you; their eyes are full of hope, just like you....If you listen real close, you can hear them whisper their legacy to you. Go on, lean in. Listen. You hear it?*

I believe the key to successfully passing on lessons learned in war resides in John Keating's words, and in our ability as teachers to point our students toward the faces and voices of the past. Those faces and voices, applied to a study of World War I, provide a dramatic and powerful way to bring that time period to life for our students. The soldiers' voices enable students to see those brave men as the sons, husbands, fathers, and friends that they were. Hearing the voices, reading about the losses their families and their countries experienced, and learning how war altered their lives forever is a compelling way to understand why war often is the last alternative for resolving conflict.

Such was the thinking that fueled my most recent technology project.

Stories of veterans of war

The same month in which much of the world was glued to television sets watching cruise missiles fall on Baghdad, a small group of my learners was holed up in my classroom preparing the Web pages that would become part of our Stories From the Street Website *http://www.masters.ab.ca/bdyck/ CyberFair1/index.html*.

For some time, those students had been uncovering the history behind the names of the streets that surround our school. Situated on a former Canadian Armed Forces base, the nearby streets are named after World War I battles Canadian soldiers played a part in. Each student had chosen a battle, researched it, and created a Web page to profile his or her findings. Those Web pages became part of our entry in the Global Schoolhouse CyberFair 2003 *http://www.gsn.org/cf/*.

That lesson might have been a purely academic activity—but it actually was so much more. Somewhere between researching the bare facts and polishing their Web pages, the students came face to face with the people behind the uniforms.

The connection didn't happen by accident. Using primary and secondary sources, students were introduced to the grim reality of war and to the people who experienced it. Sifting through audio files *http://www.archives.ca/05/0518/051801_e.html*, soldiers' diaries *http://www.vac-acc.gc.ca/general/sub.cfm?source=history/firstwar/1diary*, video footage *http://www.doctv.com/trailers/john-mccraes-war.html*, interviews with veterans *http://collections.ic.gc.ca/audio/vetinter.htm*, artwork *http://www.archives.ca/05/050801_e.html*, poetry *http://www.oucs.ox.ac.uk/ltg/projects/jtap/tutorials/intro/*, and novels set in 1914-1918 *http://redcedar.swifty.com/2002/nominees/fiction/charliewilcox.htm*, provided students with content for their Stories From the Street and helped communicate a quiet, but profound, message from another time and place.

History comes to life

I will never forget the day we read "The First of July," a World War I story by David McFarlane that is included in the book *Story of a Nation* *http://www.randomhouse.ca/features/storyofanation/book.html*. In this true story, MacFarlane tells about the summer he was assigned the task of sorting through the papers and memorabilia of an elderly spinster neighbor. To his surprise, he discovered that her past contained a World War I romance and tragedy. My students sat absolutely silent as they heard about the infamous Battle of Somme (1916) *http://www.stemnet.nf.ca/beaumont/somme2.htm*, a shocking massacre in which the First Newfoundland Regiment was virtually annihilated within 30 minutes. To commemorate this horrific attack, one student made a sound recording of *Newfoundland Park Memorial http://www.masters.ab.ca/bdyck/Diary/Quentin2/index.html*, a poem found on a plaque at the entrance to the scene of this attack.

Subsequent online fieldtrips to places like Flanders Fields and Vimy Ridge provided students with a sense of the battle settings they were writing about. After moving through those battlegrounds and trenches, all of us felt as though we had been there—we could almost touch the monuments and the walls of the trenches.

Reading the soldiers' diary entries proved to be very moving and thought provoking—and turned out to be one of the most stirring experiences of this project. Those primary source materials exposed the soldiers' fears, the horrors they endured, the challenges of trench life, the ever-present homesickness, and their dreams for the future. Each student included on his or her Web page a sound file of one story from the trenches *http://www.masters.ab.ca/bdyck/Diary/Moreuil/index.html.* As the readers of those diary entries, the students became the voices of the soldiers while recorded artillery sounds filled the background.

A tour of a local attraction, the Museum of the Regiments *http://www. museumoftheregiments.ca/,* connected students to valuable library resources and World War I experts who answered questions and shared interesting stories. We learned that the last soldier killed in World War I was a Canadian soldier who was shot just two minutes before the armistice took place in 1918. One student, a horse enthusiast, had to leave the room when one of the veterans shared the unique place that horses had in World War I battles. She told us later that seeing horses in gas masks and hearing how many of them had died made her "sick to her stomach."

"Stories From the Street" was a lesson and a project John Keating would have loved. My students took time to "lean in." They listened to the voices, and the result was some very powerful learning.

Additional Resources

History Lessons: World War I Lessons
http://ohioteach.history.ohio-state.edu/Lessons/fww.htm

These lesson plans from the History of Teaching Institute at Ohio State University are designed to help students see the effects of WWI on different segments of the population.

The Western Front—Would You Have Made a Good Officer?
http://www.activehistory.co.uk/games/ww1RF/Western Front Sim.htm

This simulation is intended to give students an idea of what World War I must have been like for those who fought it.

Life in the Trenches
http://www.activehistory.co.uk/games/trenches/frameset.htm

This online simulation will shed light on the conditions faced in the trenches.

Afterword

Certain authors, speaking of their works, say: "My book," "My commentary," "My history," etc. They resemble middle-class people who have a house of their own and always have "My house" on their tongue. They would do better to say: "Our book," "Our commentary," "Our history," etc., because there is in them usually more of other people's than their own. —Blaise Pascal

One thing I've learned about rebooting your mind is that you're never done. You see, rebooting is not a one-time accomplishment; it actually becomes your state of being. Just like my computer, my thinking or my cognitive operating system becomes sluggish and needs to be rebooted again and again. I suspect that will go on for as long as I am part of this ever-changing profession. Realizing this has stopped me from looking for a moment of completion and has caused me to willingly embrace a paradigm of ongoing professional reform.

It's also important to understand that rebooting, or changing your mental models about your teaching practices, should never be done in isolation, but closely connected to others who are also professionally "on the grow." These professional learning communities, whether they occur through books, online articles, attendance at workshops, via discussions with local teachers, professional collaboration through listserv, or personal experiences at home, are dependent on the interactions we have outside our own experience. And as Pascal aptly suggests, our thinking becomes so intertwined with the thinking of our colleagues, that in the end, we aren't quite sure where our thinking ends and theirs begins. More intriguing is the thought that this mix can become a new entity of it's own, something fresh and mighty. The words from writers like Parker Palmer, Rick Wormeli, Caroline McCullen, Janet Allen, Chris Tovani, and Deb Bambino have so thoroughly penetrated my thinking that many of my own ideas bear witness to theirs. Add to this my *Education World* editor, Gary Hopkins, who made it his business to make sure the message of my writing didn't get lost in unclear wording. Their influence on my thoughts and writing has been extensive. *Education World's* generous willingness to endorse the reissuing of my articles freed me to embark on the venture of giving these online articles a hardcopy home.

Being part of a research and development school has kept me on my toes. My administration's decision to make professional development a weekly occurrence has led me to rethink some of the sacred cows of our profession and to encounter some incommodious learning initiatives. I will always be grateful for the insistent prodding of Tom Rudmik and Doreen Grey, as they took a somewhat outdated educator like me and unleashed dreams concerning how I might create profound learning for my students and myself. Also woven within the intent of my words are the solid teaching principles modeled for me by my closest teaching colleagues, Byron Thiessen and Linda Dyck and the middle school team at Master's Academy and College.

We teach in such extraordinary times. Who would think that a group of like-minded professionals from all over the world would make it a priority to connect online every day for the purpose of mutual support and professional growth? MiddleWeb listserv has done just that, as it has become a place for teachers from one end of North America to the other, to look for best teaching practices to model and exemplify. Some of my most potent reflections came out of those online discussions, and my writing is a testimony of the powerful mentoring provided on MiddleWeb listserv for me.

The internal belief that you have something to write begins many years before putting pen to paper. This belief was a direct deposit of my parents, Alf and Annie Pettersen. The love of words and wording that fuels my writing was modeled for me in my childhood home by my dad's reflective spirit and love of reading and cheered along by my biggest advocate, my mom.

When you reboot your mind, there's always someone at home making dinner and keeping things rolling. Without my husband Ron, I wouldn't have had the time or energy to reboot my mind. He nurtures my creative spirit, frees me to write, and listens to me when writing becomes a painful process. My love and thanks to him.

Parenting my five children has taught me much more than I've ever taught them. Some of those lessons are found in this book.

Stephanie, Paul, Julia, Lindsay, John—and Paul McPhail, I am thankful for every one of you!

How do I know what I think until I see what I say? —E.M. Forster